SQUEEZED
LIGHT

OTHER BOOKS BY LISSA WOLSAK

The Garcia Family Co-Mercy, Tsunami (1994)

An Heuristic Prolusion, Friends of Runcible Mountain (2000)

Pen Chants or nth or 12 Spirit-like Impermanences, Roof Books (2000)

A Defence of Being, First Ana, Spanner (2002)

A Defence of Being, Second Ana, Wild Honey Press (2005)

Lissa
Wolsak

SQUEEZED
LIGHT

collected poems 1994–2005

Introduction by George Quasha
with Charles Stein

Station Hill
of Barrytown

Published by Station Hill Press, Inc., 120 Station Hill Road, Barrytown, NY 12507, as a project of the Institute for Publishing Arts, Inc., in Barrytown, New York, a not-for-profit, tax-exempt organization [501(c)(3)], supported in part by grants from the New York State Council on the Arts.

Grateful acknowledgment is made for permission to reprint *The Garcia Family Co-Mercy*, first published by Tsunami, Vancouver, BC (1994), "An Heuristic Prolusion," first published by Friends of Runcible Mountain, Documents in Poetics, Vancouver, BC (2000); *Pen Chants or nth or 12 Spirit-like Impermanences*, first published by Roof Books, New York, NY (2000); *A Defence of Being, First Ana*, first published by Spanner, Hereford, UK (2002); *A Defence of Being, Second Ana*, first published by Wild Honey Press, Bray, Ireland (2005).

Online catalogue: www.stationhill.org
e-mail: publishers@stationhill.org

Interior and cover design by Susan Quasha. Cover image, "change excess," by Allen Fisher. Courtesy the artist, copyright 2006 Allen Fisher.

Library of Congress Cataloging-in-Publication Data
Wolsak, Lissa.
 Squeezed light : collected poems, 1994-2005 / by Lissa Wolsak.
   p. cm.
 ISBN 978-1-58177-116-9 (alk. paper)
 I. Title.
 PR9199.3.W556S78 2010
 811'.54—dc22

                              2009045504

Manufactured in the United States of America

Acknowledgments

These texts might not have arisen but for the vivacity and dash from certain pivotal imps in the field; my gratitude to all the marvelous guides who affectionately, enduringly contributed to my reflections. For the idea and fire, thanks first to Vincentina and Steven, and to Drue Delanty, Peter O'Leary, David Bromige, Rick Pollay, and Carole Christopher, who have been especially, lovingly present throughout; to Don and Thelmar Crawford of Melody Hill, Del Mar, at whose home on a beach scarp I slept, in the embodiment of my ice-floe library, so long ago. To Betty Lambert, whom I miss like mad; also to Colin Browne, Ralph Maud, and Pierre Coupey, for each nudged me toward certain authorial wonders. Fervent thanks to all who engagingly, graciously extended invitations and welcome: Randolph Healy, Allen Fisher, Nate Dorward, Jack Kimball, Drew Milne, Jake Berry, Catriona Strang, Lisa Robertson, Laynie Brown, Thomas Evans, Lisa Jarnot, Susan Schultz, James Sherry, Kevin Nolan, Lawrence Upton, Barry McKinnon, Stephen Collis, Leslie Scalapino, Hank Lazer, Susan Clark, David Dowker, Louis Cabri, Pete Smith, Jeanne Heuving, Henry Gould, Elizabeth Robinson, Cynthia Hogue, Leonard Schwartz, Erin Moure, David Ayre, Deanna Ferguson, Mike Barnholden, Douglas Oliver, Alice Notley, Trevor Joyce, Jeff Derksen, Jen Hofer, Andrea Brady, Keston Sutherland, Aaron Vidaver, Roger Farr, Steve Ward, Jenny Penberthy, Alan Clements, Kerri Sonnenberg, Christine Stewart, Miles Champion, Rob Holloway, Kent Johnson, Tom Beckett, Robert Mittenthal, Charles Altieri, Jocelyn Saidenberg, Miekal And.

I also wish to thank the editors of Tsunami, Friends of Runcible Mountain, Roof Books, *Writing Magazine*, *Front*, *Conundrum*, Spanner, Wild Honey Press, *Onedit*, Lounge at Dard, *Tolling Elves*, *Alterra*, Gorse Press, *Green Stone Mountain Review*, *Cambridge Conference of Contemporay Poetry Review*, TinFish, The Gig, *Matrix*, *INTERFACES ~ University of Paris*, College of the Holy Cross, *Barscheit Nation*, O Books, Barque Press, *How2*, *The East Village*, *9th St. Labs*, *PennSound*, *Raddle Moon*, *The Capilano Review*, and *Open Text Anthology*, in which the works in this volume first appeared.

My deepest gratitude goes to George Quasha, Charles Stein, Susan Quasha, and Jenny Fox for their unfailing support, their genuine interest, humanity, and integrity.

That I was searingly, scintillatingly led here, is a perpetual surprise to me.

VANCOUVER, B.C.
December 3, 2009

Contents

for my friend

INTRODUCTION

Squeezed Coherence

I

We have here a body of work at home in its own elusiveness. Language sculpture? That's one possible, though unlikely, name for what we find here, about which it can be said: it carves into time, as if, in the actual time of writing, poetic process had incised directly into "time matter," cutting through to undisclosed layers of *undertime*. Or, from another angle of experience: once inside this elusive work, this *unfolding language substance*—feeling its attractions (some strange, all at least partly not-yet-known)—one senses a multidirectional crossflow: so much is happening from moment to moment, so much is coming through, one hardly knows where to stand. Quite clearly the poet has chosen her words at a level resistant to immediate thought, no doubt in part for their musics, their senses, and their sensualities.

> I insculpt
> the gasp of individual perception

Lissa Wolsak tells us so much and in so many ways that there is no central focus. She holds us, it seems, in a sort of split perspective—a *perspectival doubling*—that challenges readerly identity even as it forms, and she does this by keeping us inside poetic movement while pushing us out to one edge or another, instant by instant. It can require a radical bi-focal reading, a manifold awareness rippling through the poem; pulling in and keeping out, welcoming and alienating. The reader might imagine it to be somewhat like *rafting the rapids* (to metaphorically extend an element from *The Garcia Family Co-Mercy*) while simultaneously standing on the riverbank watching the flow, verbal things passing, angling in the recall of how to civilize at a far periphery.

Yet she does invoke, among these felt perspectives, certain near-recurrences, instances of special attention:

> Quantum physics engages the term 'qualia,' defined as, those
> temporary states flagging our 'immediate' reality..."no more
> than dispositions...things that can float free." The "redness

of red, the painfulness of pain." The whatness .. that which
gives things qualities. Qualia are *the* essential feature of
consciousness.

("An Heuristic Prolusion")

Implicit here is a curve of her poetics, an aspect, as it were, of *qualia poet-
ics*, which allows for a certain unexplainable and irreducible singularity in
direct experience through language. The inconclusive debates in philosophy of
mind, epistemology, consciousness studies, and artificial intelligence—as
to whether qualia even exist—are not in play here; their force is mainly
academic, but, in terms of Wolsak's poetics, argument as such seems largely
inconsequential. Here is a principle of another kind, whose scholarly par-
ticularism by no means skips intelligence and discriminating awareness.

A work so deeply founded in principle sees its insights and discoveries in
multiple frames, on separable planes, and with variable functions. It views in
compounds and linkages—aesthetic-sensuous, interpersonal-social...—in-
stances of what finds a working name, "co-mercy," "the art of harmlessness"

> where the same relation may be observed throughout the whole
> universe, where significance "bleeds into an unconstrainable
> chain."

The statement that a work has a poetics can be seen as indicating a con-
tinuum. It would mean, on the one hand, a self-evident notion applicable
to any realized poem or, indeed, any intentional discursive act, that there is
something that makes it hold together; and, on the other hand, a self-con-
scious operative *principle of singular coherence*. (And among the latter there could
be another range of distinctions reflecting the degree of self-consciousness
in furthering the core principle and its extent of operation.) Yet it is no
longer strange for a poet to embody both ends of the continuum (if it ever
really was so strange—think of Chaucer); that is, consciously seeking out,
as a matter of principle, the hidden integrities of actual speech (including
"found" speech), language as it happens in life and develops in text, yet ren-
dering it in a further order of attention that generates an unknown coher-
ence, revealing possibilities intrinsic to language. Such might be a starting
point for Lissa Wolsak.

II

We could begin an assessment of her work virtually anywhere along the continuum, because there is no correct approach, no main angle, no right place in poetic history to which she belongs. As a poet whose real work begins relatively late in life (like Charles Olson in this respect), she has *only* mature work; she creates an oeuvre from the start. No juvenilia in evidence. No manifest process of development. No imitations and no extensions of literary/poetic precedent. This is not to say that she has not worked at every point in a conscious relation to "tradition" (in a sense residually relatable to T.S. Eliot's "Tradition and the Individual Talent," minus the attachment to a dominant Western tradition). On the contrary, as can be seen in her collected poems here, her intensive connection to a range of poetic modalities and letters in general, rather than positioning her as "belated" in a lineage of mastery, frees her to choose a path both resonant with poetic relations and clear in its actual singularity.

She's a poet everywhere tracking the emergence of a poetic principle. At one level everything she engages is a work in poetics to the extent that it moves intentionally through reflection of its *own* principle. To discover her poetics one participates equally in the poetry and her writing about it, if indeed her key statement, "An Heuristic Prolusion," can be said to be "about" her work as such; no doubt her statements of and about poetics are themselves performative of that of which they speak. In a related way, Robert Duncan spoke of his own work and that of Charles Olson as requiring that one read that work—all manifestations of the work—at the level of their poetics. And poetics in their sense embodied a full-scale view of reality—indeed a vision of, for instance, the "human universe" (Olson) or the "open universe" (Duncan).

Poetics for such poets indeed discovers itself through the technical, formal, stylistic, and compositional considerations behind their work, yet it also involves the very foundational principles by which a vision of reality constitutes itself at any and every level. If poetry is the "visionary vehicle," Blake's "Chariot of Genius," then poetics might be the intuitive design and also the processual means by which it moves forward—and beyond itself. And this *beyond* might require that poetics be not only a constructive principle but the contrary, however one would characterize that. Maybe Wallace

Stevens' "Poetry is a Destructive Force" is tonally out of register ("like a man / In the body of a violent beast")—but maybe not entirely: "I want to work within or near consciousness-collapsing events." ("An Heuristic Prolusion")

Such a notion of taking things apart can have a range of nuances, not always easy to specify. Destructing (after Heidegger's *Destruktion* and including of course *deconstruction*)—de(re)structuring—further structuring. It can have a lot to do with how language comes to its possibilities. And how it serves the complexity of one's actual experience and activity of mind—by letting the intricate forces find their way in the poem under hand. Being *in* time, language takes up its own time, right *at* the time.

III

Almost any interesting poetry can expose questions about the nature of time—mostly unanswerable questions, yet necessary ones that keep us in touch with the impermanent "constructions" we live by. But these questions are hardly in the foreground of attention. In a certain sense all art forms suspend time or transmute it into non-clock time, co-opting its flow by way of intentional/constructed "art time." Some poetry does this with radical intentionality by suspending the directionality and spacing of reading/ listening time. It opens a threshold between time and non-time, or the temporal and the atemporal, by urging the mind into a time of its own, a self-conscious timing sense. To mention it here is to directly emphasize what certain poets already carry out indirectly. There are poets, in fact, whose re-temporalizing constructs open singular perspectives on time, or make time seem to reflect its own artificiality—an arti*factual* reflection that's rather like self-reflection put into orbit.

Lissa Wolsak brings intimacy to the disruption of time. Its sudden eros in sensuous fragmentation instantly embraces what it scatters. You can almost feel her breath still clinging to a partially released phrase. So much is let loose in the flow of the text, so many different self-asserting entities of speech rising into the readerly audium, yet not much comes out whole-bodied. A theme may show itself with the arhythmic display of apples falling from a tree, a ripe one here, a riper one there. We may never come to see the tree. We know in any given poem that a trunk or some other organismic spread is operative, whether rooted or rhizomatic, but we know it by circumvolent soundings: whirrs and thumps; cracks; musical twisters; vocal incursions.

The scattered limbs, the poetic parts, come together only in the mind of the engaged reader—the poem-entracked, -enrouted mind, whose journey through the work is itself a *configuration of the text*. It's as though this process elicits from the reader a more intense responsibility in performing the text at the level of its integrity—a responsive engagement in a polyvalent field. The poetic has an immediate function—*leading*. It guides toward configurative happening, recurrently regathering the limbs of the text. (Osiris reconstituted in every move of the poem—by reading one back to oneself.) Whatever this poetic process takes apart—the logic of rational projection, history, politics, myth . . .—is subject to *open-spacing*, which creates the condition for sudden configurative flashes, and renders them clear and vivid. And in the newly open-spaced field, each vivification is now a spark point for yet another space arousal, an axis of a new beginning—a place inspired with the speaking breath, as if the lingual site recited itself.[1]

The grit and traction of such a site is often first of all a *cut* through familiar discourse, which implicitly lays bare certain limitations behind the silencing of self-true speaking. ("I speak as one silenced," begins "An Heuristic Prolusion.") The very act of partial or altered citation, as a recurrent fact of composition, offers critical or even analytical focus, a taking apart in process that is also an opening, allowing unaccountable accords with possible saying. In this way composition also comprises multiple acts of *de*composition in the "formation" of a moving field of flashes and weaves.

---

[1] We borrow this notion from Gary Hill's single-channel video *Site Recite (a prologue)* (1989), in which the artist brings in and out of focus certain strangely arrayed and rather mysterious objects, shifting suddenly on a flat circular surface, and treats them as *sites* of language where a voice recites the words of a rich and mysterious text. The recited text and the articulated place together configure a singular poetics. See G. Quasha and C. Stein, *An Art of Limina: Gary Hill's Works and Writings*, Foreword by Lynne Cooke (Barcelona: Ediciones Polígrafa, 2009). The video can be viewed at www.garyhill.com.

IV

Composition unfolds through *field reflexivity*. In such practice the underlying force of coherence is a species of activated poetic faith in which attention is somehow double-visioned to include both *center* (the verbal "object" in immediate focus) and *periphery* (the fluid context emerging in process). (We mentioned above the perspectival doubling signaled by the poet's earliest work, *The Garcia Family Co-Mercy*, which opens this collection.) Objects in the field "relate" in mysterious ways, but whatever the way, it's non-hierarchical, barely narratological, and "rational" only by an unexampled "logic" of possibility and singularity. Yet even to speak of a logic is to say too much, to impose lofty justification for something already complete in itself, and hardly in need of further lift.

Poetics, to get its bearings here, may have to abandon literary history, at least temporarily, in favor of discovering an operative poetic principle on grounds other than what might be available by precedent. Eventually one may have to do so by way of the *poetics of principle* itself, explored through provisional perspectives, invoking the spirit of Blake's "Anything possible to be believed is an image of the truth," yet following the poem to the heart of things. We can think both Wallace Stevens—"The accuracy of accurate letters is an accuracy with respect to the structure of reality"— and Jackson Mac Low—applying *mimesis* as "the imitation of nature in its *mode of operation.*"

The focus here is on a certain quality of *field awareness.* Since Charles Olson's "composition by field" ("Projective Verse," 1950), there clearly have been many approaches with some relation to his generative insights, approaches that, like Olson's own poetics, are in part retrospective (to Pound's *Pisan Cantos,* Williams' *Paterson*) and yet original to emerging work. Lissa Wolsak's work, the ear that hears relations, certainly draws from this poetic stream, amongst others. And yet at every point it speaks so definingly for itself that one is ever faced with characterizing what seems to retreat from definition. Its hold on the field, its power to churn energies at large, resides both in the particulars and in the space that opens out from them. *Saying*, as it were, is at sea, where things said are definite objects set free, which in turn beacon back to directing attention further, to an immediate elsewhere. What is past, the previous, has no authority but resonance. What is retained carries forward mainly as a certain aura.[2]

V

Things said have the force they do in the moment of saying; something concrete is handed over. Yet, immediately, another significance rises into view, another sense of the phrase's en-nested-ness, say, in phrases gone before, another set of signifying relations. There is a movement here of a compelling sort, that will not lend itself to precise determination, if only (but not only) because it is each determination that sets the thing in motion.

All of this is occurring in real time—the verse geared not of course to a meter or set of procedures/parameters but to the unfolding speaking as the occurrence of the text—*listened to* and *through* within the emerging field. And yet "real time" here does not become a constant in its own medium, the medium at hand, as might be in the case of video or film (the same in each replay), because here the experienced time is a function of a particular act

---

[2] The question of "aura" in works of art and in poetry is perhaps in need of some further reflection since Walter Benjamin's famous declaration in "The Work of Art in the Age of Mechanical Reproduction" to the effect that the aura associated with the material being of works of art has been dissipated because of the facility by which art works can be copied and distributed. Certainly that facility has been enhanced vastly in our electronic age, yet many artists since, say, the 1960s have worked with reproducible aspects of artistic production, concentrating on the resonant or non-resonant qualities of the various media themselves, often manifesting the magic of their individual works on those terms. Indeed, in the case of writing, the mechanical reproducibility of the text (hardly new in modernity) has only served to highlight singular acts of reading, where the aura may be reconstituted and lost and reconstituted again right in one's engagement with a text such as Wolsak's. Where the principle of writing and the principle of reality are equally found in the acts by which the meaning of the work and the nature of reality are configured, the aura, in the sense of qualities experienced as belonging to the field under configuration, can hardly be discounted.

of reading—the reader's, which *includes* the poet's as reader/*re*reader. Reading is a variable.[3]

So there is *actual time*, reading time. This is a singular act. While such unique timing may in some degree always be the case in reading, the difference here, in Lissa Wolsak, is that the verse directly attends this unstable time as the *real* one, the real *real time*, as it were—a concrete actual forward-moving *open* time. A created time that is actual, actually the case, inside reading. The emphasis is not on the created object that may come to hang constant in the gallery of hierarchizing attention, but on things hanging in the air in listening space—blowing with the breeze, following the breath.

Now, there is something important here that cannot quite be said: the breathing in the verse attracts a readerly breath, *a further breathing*. Inspiration, so it seems, draws into *conspiration*, textually. There is a synchrony that is also synergy. A co-performativity: unfolding events in language are registered not only cognitively but—well, we hesitate, because any term here risks over-concretizing something liminal to psyche and actual body. The singular time-event occurs as a co-creative oscillation between text and reader, and accordingly the event is registered both at the threshold of mind and body and *as itself a threshold*. The reading itself, as *limen*, opening upon (to use Olson's words) the *further nature* of the poem.

VI

The activated threshold, the vibratile limen within reading, creates it own sense of space. The challenging notion of "time-space," even as a continuum, has a particular coherence inside reading, and most particularly reading made conscious of its configurative responsibility. The poetics we have been drawing upon here inherently understands the time-space notion, one might say, as mutually self-modifying: time refocuses space, and space, time. Focus on the one calls the other into play. Into intensive process.

One wonders if it would ever be possible, or even desirable, to have a stable or consistent notion of time *or* space. How they appear to be, in a

---

[3] A poet can read her work very differently over time, or may seem to outgrow a poem (as say Auden did, disastrously returning to earlier work as destroyer-reviser). Robert Duncan's re-embrace of early work in *The Years As Catches: First poems (1939-1946)* (Berkeley: Oyez, 1966) is a remarkable instance of an inclusive expansion *back* to an earlier poetics.

Wolsak text, is a function of a between. In many senses. And here is one of the places where this register of poetics may be said to contribute to a revisioning of "reality." Whether viewed as temporalized space or spatialized time, it brings forward the liminality of space and time, which may be the experienceable aspect of the time-space concept—that we are literally caught in the middle. The torsional journey *between* motivates an originary articulation within language, which cuts through space (the page) and edges time toward a mercurial *outside* (voice)—vocalized intensities.

Intensity? No doubt one of the possible definitions of poetry is intensified discourse—or, rather, self-intensifying discourse. But whence this intensity? The question returns us to the sense of poetics that addresses technique, rhetoric, form, etc. What's interesting in this regard about Wolsak's poetics is that the issue of *concrete means* and the discovery and actualization of a *view of reality* are synchronous/synergistic, co-performative, and operative on the same plane.

VII

We have mentioned Wolsak's connection with a lineage, one could say tradition, of intentional poetics in, for instance, Olson's and Duncan's requiring that a reader engage their work in poetry at the level of their poetics; one could add any number of precedents—Gertrude Stein, Mallarmé, indeed William Blake! But we can also look beyond poetry as such to a practice of conscious language amongst those who attempt "impossible speech."[4] We have noted

---

[4] Of course "beyond poetry as such" has many ranges relevant here, including, say, a Laura Riding's "break[ing] the spell of poetry," Samuel Beckett's "subtraction" as "nonknower/no-can-doer," Maurice Blanchot's "récits," Buckminster Fuller's "mental mouthfuls," John Cage's "lectures" (plus "unfocus"), Edmond Jabès' "books," David Antin's "talking," Franz Kamin's "psychotopological diversions," Gary Hill's "videograms" and "electronic linguistics," and so on. We are very aware of the complexity of noting that Wolsak is working within a manifold lineage/tradition (which we are *not* attempting to define here), particularly since it continues to be fully alive and intricately webbed; and we know that our way of characterizing this or that aspect of the work and thought can seem applicable as well to certain other poets: particular sentences could be addressing the work of Robert Kelly, Kenneth Irby, Gerrit Lansing, Clark Coolidge, Susan Howe.... But the point is neither to claim exclusivity nor to compile a corresponding "list," and certainly not comparison, invidious or otherwise. We acknowledge the perils of discriminating distinctions and the challenge of presenting singularity in poetics.

Wolsak's "I speak as one silenced"; she also cites Michel de Certeau's "Why write, if not in the name of impossible speech?" And she quotes Maimonides:

> the prophets use in their speeches ... equivocal words and
> words that are not intended to mean what they indicate,
> according to their first signification....

This connects her with the practice of apophasis—what is usually called "negative saying" (as in "negative theology") but which Michael Sells corrects to *unsaying*.[5] We would suggest yet another refinement in the distinction: the apophatic points away from fixed indication of meaning and toward a *further saying*. The energizing state of discourse, beyond fixation, is to be speaking further than the last thing said or thought. This further speaking might simply be what an attentive reader configures in her hearing as she receives the text. As such, it may or may not correspond to processes of thinking with which the poet might identify, an issue of some importance in much literary interpretation. Yet the poetic apophasis that we are addressing as *furthering* knows that its opening extends beyond interpretation as such, the poet's as much as the reader's. Poet and reader are in a certain sense equal in being carried forward—or might we say, honoring the non-linearity of the process, *outward.*

VIII

The means by which such furthering is brought about is never fixed but is a function of its singular operation in the readerly event. One could perhaps say a lot about Wolsak's self-interrupting process; her quasi-neologistic

---

[5] *Mystical Languages of Unsaying* (Chicago: The University of Chicago, 1994), a remarkable study of apophasis in Plotinus, John the Scot Eriugena, Ibn 'Arabi, Marguerite Porete, and Meister Eckhart, which engages them at the level of their poetics. Accordingly Sells' work is a contribution to what we have been calling the *poetics of thinking*, which is not to foreground the possible link between poetry and thinking (even their possible interchangeability), as Heidegger does, but that a given *thinking* may be known *in terms of* a poetics, or perhaps as *implying* a poetics. That a thinking has a signature, as an art or poetry does (or as a voice has an identity), is registered as a fact of the language through which we know it. This approach may offer a further sense in which thinking and poetry are connected—as *singularities.*

resuscitation of strange, arcane, archaic, even technical words in alien contexts; her rhetorics and sonorities divagating in textual tangles, crisscrossing in musics of their own invention. But this is not the place to risk interfering (by way of extended interpretation) with a process that refuses to stand outside itself in cognitive relief. No breathers for the academic mind (especially one's own).

The text converses with itself to make space for reading. In fact, reading is what it's already doing, by way of textual self-dialogue and inquiry into the roots of its own conception. In the very density of the text is an always unknown kind of spaciousness. Perhaps something like this is carried by the Japanese word *ma*[6] which can be rendered as space, time, gap, emptiness, negative space, or the space (time) between structural parts.

When a text spatializes itself by disjunction and furtherance of inquiry, it charges the space between any still activated elements. Saying, unsaying, resaying, further saying—the process creates a meaning-saturating open-spacing that can range, experientially, from free-fall to stop-time and time out. The poem itself may serve as limen between temporal and atemporal. It would be a site in which a fall from time seems to reverse something we take to be primordial—the fall *into* time. Such a reversal, a *metanoia*, initiates a fundamental re-orientation—a still point and, therein, a refocusing toward what could be called *fortunate focus*. Analogue of fortunate fall/*feliz culpa*, it stands for the unspeakable happiness possible precisely inside creation. *Malgré tout.*

---

[6] In *The Art of Looking Sideways*, Alan Fletcher writes: "Space is substance. Cézanne painted and modeled space. Giacometti sculpted by 'taking the fat off space.' Mallarmé conceived poems with absences as well as words. Ralph Richardson asserted that acting lay in pauses.... Isaac Stern described music as 'that little bit between each note—silences which give the form....' The Japanese have a word (*ma*) for this interval which gives shape to the whole. In the West we have neither word nor term. A serious omission." (Phaidon: London, 370) See especially Kunio Komparu's great work, *The Noh Theater: Principles and Perspectives*, "Time and Space in Noh: Apposition and Fusion," Chapter Seven (New York: Weatherhill/Tankosha, 1983), pp. 70-95.

IX

Saying and unsaying are continuous in the work here, and indeed can happen nearly simultaneously or at the same site in syntax. Even the title of this collection, *Squeezed Light,* compacts in two words various meaning possibilities and has polyvalent force. A technical term from physics, "squeezed light" requires fairly advanced math to understand fully, but in the raw, so to speak, it's richly suggestive. On the important scientific applications of the concept, one website starts out: "Can light be squeezed? In fact it is the *quantum noise* of light that can be squeezed. Such *squeezed light* (a squeezed state of light) is a special form of light that is researched in the field of quantum optics."[7] Obviously the poet occupies a zone of resonance that takes very little from the actual science in the immediate order of meaning—and right from the start, we're already inside the poem in saying its name. Its title: standing in the fore of the book, it first of all *images*—a coloring (senses of *squeeze*) in waves of suggestive connections, hardly (for the majority, one assumes, of readers) indicating science. That comes in a remove from image-power as such—an unsaying to make space for an uncertain *other* saying, a definition in physics that most readers can scarcely reach into. We play with the metaphoric ranges of its saying. We think it part way. And stop where we stop.

The title is its own field, and holds the poetics with a sharp indeterminacy—a saying that is already an unsaying, yet still unfolds. Like many words or definite phrases in the poems, it can indicate a (partially hidden) sentence, an extending domain, an entire but incompletely available phenomenon, a fragmented discussion of possibility, a speculation about

---

[7] The Albert-Einstein-Institut Legal Press: www.squeezed-light.de. A formal (but still non-mathematical) definition involves statements like this: "Squeezed light is produced when quantum noise in one or the other of two complementary variables describing a light beam (such as phase and amplitude) is greatly reduced at the expense of the other by sending the light through (a series of) special optical crystals." For extended definition see American Institute of Physics: "Inside Science Research—Physics News Update," Number 784 #2, July 7, 2006 by Phil Schewe and Ben Stein: www.aip.org/pnu/. Quick mathematical definitions can be searched online as "squeezed coherent state."

measure, a reflection turned back on itself as collection of poetry—and more. Its immediate metaphoric purchase might seem to characterize the highly wrought texture of Wolsak's verse itself, and at the same time the physics term sits back in pristine scientism, a *footing* presumed to be real, yet which for the uninitiated amounts to inaccessibility. Something real but not quite fully said—or spoken as by one silenced.

X

A word means what it means in the place we find it, and yet it is both unsaid and said further by resonance with something else—connecting with an actual *elsewhere* rendered ambivalent in its identity, its very self-sameness. This *field effect* of resonant language uncovers *non-locality* as poetic phenomenon, a metaphoric sense of the physics term indicating a direct influence of one object on another object at some distance, in violation of the principle of locality.[8] (LW: "... the mind is non-local....")

Yet perhaps "non-locality" and "direct influence" are also a bit misleading as terms, in that any given event is *experientially local* to itself (however connected to others), and simultaneous separate but connected events may well be neither direct nor accountably influenced. We might more usefully consider such events as instances of *further locality*, extending the very sense/sensoriality of place, and dynamically *radial* in formation. Such an approach may relieve us of the need to account for what thrives beyond description, minus even the illusion that physics or any hard science can save us from (uncomfortably necessary) unknowing. Lissa Wolsak inhabits a living principle of (self-)formation, and her own poetics furthers the force of *local* in

---

[8] LW (email 8.4.09) offers this confirming connection on non-locality and squeezed light: "The amplitude and phase of electromagnetic fields such as light are subject to intrinsic quantum fluctuations. By 'squeezing' the light (using sophisticated spectroscopic techniques) the uncertainty in the field amplitude can be reduced below the 'quantum noise level' by a Heisenberg trade-off with the uncertainty in the frequency. The photons produced in squeezed light experiments have strong non-local correlations that cannot be explained by conventional semi-classical electromagnetic theory." *Physics Today* (1997) If one had a chance to rename "non-locality," perhaps the better term would be *hyper-locality*.

the complexity of *field*, registered as: "The pressure/horror and the beauty of Being .. everywhere at once."[9]

<h1 style="text-align:center">XI</h1>

Like the title, many words and sometime terms seem to remain in a partial state of reclusion. For example, *who*, we wonder at the start of *Pen Chants*, is Na Carminagua? (One suspects that, unlike Pound's *Cantos*, an annotated index of references and special terms would not help all that much, and indeed, if monumentalized as Index à la *Cantos*, might even be misleading or distracting as a divergence from implied terms of free readership.[10]) Each unclear meaning is its own unsaying—yet it retains a hint, a hope of saying *something*. However unattested or open the meaning-site, it radiates to its own effect. Each (relatively) clear meaning is unsaid by the next, only to be further said, retaining past meaning as resonance—an enrichment of aura and, it might seem, a *squeezing* of aura. A confluence of meanings at a single site jumps time to a radial, rather than sequential, perspective.

The implicit poetics draws upon and extends a truth of semantic complexity, namely, that it is inherently radial: meanings come up hyper-locally

---

[9] From the above email, in which she also cites the great master of apophasis, Meister Eckhart: "When a soul wishes to experience something, she throws an image of the experience out before her and enters into her own image."

[10] Pound had a cultural agenda, and references are to key historical/cultural facts and sources; one is meant to know them or find them out in the spirit of cultural renewal (e.g., via EP's own commentary, like *Guide to Kulchur* [1938]). Wolsak is not promoting culture as such (and certainly not doctrine, least of all *religion*), but a state of mind, awareness, and poetics. Thus we might gloss Na Carminagua as, say, a minor Catholic loyalist (Raymonde Azéma) in the repression of the Cathars in 13-14th century Provence (Montaillou), but, aside from affirming a pervasive historical interest, it doesn't particularly add to the force of the poem, and, indeed, can be misleading; puzzle-solving is not a suggested path to right reading. The poet is not, for instance, siding with Catholics against heretics; indeed, she seems not to read Na Carminagua as having done so either, but somehow to stand beyond such preference. If she achieves symbolic status, it's as a *symbol of variable reference*. Compare *The Yellow Cross: The Story of the Last Cathars' Rebellion Against the Inquisition, 1290-1329*, René Weis (New York: Random House, 2002), p. 31. Wolsak's source is the celebrated work by historian Emmanuel Le Roy Ladurie, *Montaillou: The Promised Land of Error*, transl. Barbara Bray (New York: Braziller, 1978).

in the temporal process of reading, connect round about in memory, and continue asynchronously in researches and subsequent reading. Wolsak often chooses *packed* words that unfold in relational process, and once in play tend to circulate, suddenly returning in a sort of boomerang effect. We call this ambi-valencing process *axiality,* an inherent property of language brought forward, a primary openness to new inflection in use, such that it lets language evolve toward possibility as singular instantiation.

Thus a *possible path* (not a required one) through Wolsak's work is searching word meanings, which would seem to follow a practice in her own relation to words—a practice motivated by *affection* for words, an amorous relation to language that verges into the sensual and erotic. An example of her variable semantic play—its affect of infused qualia, or what might be called *open semiosis*—is the word *ana,* used in "A Defence of Being" as part title: "First Ana," "Second Ana." This usage follows one convention of *ana* as "section" of a written work; but there are many others that a simple internet search reveals.[11] One might come to a sense of "ana" almost as a feminine entity and a name used in invocation there at the start of the "defence of being"—an unfamiliar word that feels more like a name for a living being than a thing. Perhaps it signals an actual *life* in language, language that is being asked to speak for being. Is "ana" for "A Defence of Being" what "Na Carminagua" is for "Pen Chants"—a word-entity with a past (etymology, usages, history) that speaks beyond its origin, indeed *unsaying* its origin, as veritable living entity creating a *further* history, here at the *head* of the poem, in the place on the page, before reading, in the uninterpreted and elusive poem?

What one makes of this verbal site of variable reference is a readerly configuration, as indeed we have just been doing. The very opening of that site to intensified and asymmetrical activity creates *ma*—a between of meanings—a pregnant space of temporal force and, all at once, a still point. Squeezed time. Squeezed reading.

---

[11] Wolsak has alerted us to meanings not obvious without searching: (1) a direction in the 4th spatial dimension [math/geometry]; (2) Chaldean: the invisible heaven, the astral light, the heavenly mother of the terrestrial sea, and one of the triad comprising the goddesses Ana, Belita, Damkina; (3) Greek prefix for 'up'; and (4) a 'hole' or opening in a Japanese tsuba [sword guard]; among others.

XII

This state of the text invites a sense of suddenness in the arousal of language. (Suddenness here should be distinguished from mere quickness; it retains a fullness of time inside it.) We find the poet saying in her primary statement of a poetics, "An Heuristic Prolusion":

> I take occasions of experience to be related to quantum events
> ... sudden and significant. Mind arises as an infinite expression,
> pan-experiential and permeated by proto-experiences. I want to
> work within or near consciousness-collapsing events.

There is the sense of edge, of the precarious poise at the ridge of emergence, as if a sudden (yet anticipated, because intentional) language presence arrives at a wave crest—a zone of uncontrolled potential for extension, and at the same moment subject to precipitous decline—"within or near consciousness-collapsing events." If what we consider to be ordinary consciousness is held in place by context and consensus, then the intense manifestation of ontological singularity may be served by a tear in the interpreted surface. Wolsak signals a poetics of strategic shifts and variability:

> Incarnations of the shaping spirit, with generous and agile
> hermeneutics, turn the flat surface of primary understanding
> to elicit infinitivity, even if in struggle with all the confusions
> of verbal theory. The way to the hidden or deeper meaning
> of the Torah is to take a passage out of context, to find,
> if not the conglomerates of the physical formations, then
> the conglomerates of divine formations. A fundamental
> methodological principle in connection with the interpretation
> of prophecy is the deliberate violation of context as a way of
> coming to appreciate the meaning of the text. Consciousness
> breaks with its own imaginative skeleton to exist inside and
> outside the manner of things and can inquire through matter,
> energy, space..time, in anti-totalitarian postulates to the

impinging nakedness and origins. Each dream follows the mouth.[12]

These shifts have apophatic force, where each thing said or indicated gives way or gives birth to its other, producing not so much a contrary as a radical furtherance. We have seen this as an instance of *axial poetics*, an art of putting necessary things before the mind in a mind-degradable field. The aim is to achieve an appropriate performative intensity.

The poetics of performative intensity in this sense is rather different from the way poetics recognizes and holds value in general. Historically the role of poetics, as applied to the ways and means of poetry, is indeed with a view to intensification. One view of the progression of modernist poetics might be intensification through stripping away of rhetorical conventions and replacement with innovative, including indirect, strategies of enhancement. A difference with Wolsak's verse, in this context, would be the degree to which it releases identifiable rhetorics/intensifiers even as they show up—released apophatically in immediate *further saying*. They are process-degraded, recycled, returned to the ground of saying.

This amounts to a subtle but very powerful difference of view: intensification as what suddenly, spontaneously breaks through cracks in the mask, issuing from the obscured or ignored always already intense reality. One could see it as a sort of minimalist-optimalist furtherance of Blake's cleansing the doors of perception (and of language!) so that "every thing would appear to man as it is, infinite." This is a view that comes not from assertive, kataphatic, or constructivist theory and practice, but of a certain

---

[12] This approach to language, hermeneutics, origins, mystical texts of the past *as text*—and the implicit poetics thereof—finds resonance and a vast further exploration in the works of Elliot R. Wolfson, as Wolsak herself has discovered (subsequent to the works in the present volume). Wolfson foregrounds many aspects of apophasis as intrinsic to poetics in both the narrowest and broadest senses—an unprecedented exploration that focuses within an extraordinary number of ancient, modern and contemporary precedents. See especially: *Pathwings: Philosophic & Poetic Reflections on the Hermeneutics of Time & Language*, Foreword by Charles Stein, Postface by Barbara E. Galli (Barrytown, New York: Barrytown/Station Hill Press, 2004); and *Language, Eros, Being: Kabbalistic Hermeneutics and Poetic Imagination* (New York: Fordham University Press, 2005).

non-abstinent relieving of the transcendence-reflex. A liminalizing poetics that poises, with available energy, at the threshold between charge and release. Its operative poetic principle here, always in process, realizes its own singularly squeezed coherent state.

GEORGE QUASHA
with Charles Stein
Barrytown, New York

The Garcia Family Co-Mercy

Girl   with vase of odors

cradle   one's own head . .

squinches, pendentives,   oculi, groin

cri imaginaire   pity

the river myth

was there ever

a father field

proprio   motu

fess

a hum . .

      snide, pestered

flower of the pistachio

Levinas and the elephant   slipcase

sum   him

bird-   woman

the bed will murmur

primatif . . .   faulturi

visuelle . . .

the angel

stockpiles

boatmen,   vials of

    fraidy

        cineaste

          or mumming the

egg proper

to grunt   often

I made him   secrete himself

         hunch

         back

swerve word   with

silence at its core

steepest ancestral grasses

         countries

wrapped in cloth,

so   dense

we had to go under

and   walk

rehabilitate   an   otter

eagles   cost   more

ossa   torsion

thrush   us

slept   seven years   fission

and   private

eel   in   repose

wavered   at   the   sight

               a   motherlessness,

                    raft story

          river of seed

thirst   mirari,   water slips

               from   the   needle

abaissement

flic   flac

lubricious flews   fleer

enravished   phizog

nonce

did   comas

hence a halo

by relay   portresse

a gliding   glinn

such tombs . .

rivers and shoes

      glissade . .

strand me . . loquacious, whippy

loquat   glance act

    of lofting

        fig showers

cause to stare

farrago   and disorderly

Crimea   a   blanketfull

        of smallpox

[ptarmigan

the liveliness   of divorce

harbor . .   in lime

resembles   night

and moving them   new

lion   forms

snowbird

trust

slake   at the Wimpy Bar . . . . .

spoke of   empty

delight

Florentine   groundlings

contain   half images

of the Buddha

eye and robe mingle

I would not have

          had that laugh

attract   your

insect partner

simian   pipe-off

in   extenso

wind   farm

upper   room

porno wins

speech   set

in   the   river

de vue

pataphysique

        ape-ware

           cheek pieces

              graded slate

came to be

birds

for their cloaks   kapu

depend   from the trunk

rice bird

cattle   egret

if you would only

sip   struck

glance

when I did

lies of origin

        avoid speaking . . . . . the

new thing is to skip

generations

licks like   before   while

within   sometimes I   or we

here and now . . . . . dry land rose

speaking   starvatious   you may

peer in   the nylon pool

gulley   gulch

someone hadn't   claimed

        their animal

pin curl   furl

               sou-dust

vacant   link   or not

good fur   bad fur

errant   red currants

                adversaria

       adversaria

         fresh

      elephants . . . . . .

abet   arrhythmic

      armadillos   trace

with   a   breathing

chimps   cannot swim or

                              even float

      pneumatic loaves

unsayable   foregoing   Borneoian

                              show dollars

weird-eerie   nazgul

      dominion   virtues

      grow radish

host   country   electrical

lap against

descendental   human voice

held·

us up

butterflies   drink . .

specie   amnesia   sorrowful

wildebeest   on the pan

elephants smart enough

to break   their teeth

hovered heart   as is

earshot   tong   tuft   dim

spoonshaped   leaves

of   such a trellis   or shutter

or blind   as permits one

                        gust

                wisteria,   ginger . .

                thinned off the hill

the ark I· hermeneuticized,

hoisted and withered city

Navarra   was password

had hung   asleep

in the obscuration

separate bird / morning

the palace nectarine

fell   from the pyramid

I should wolf   on the cheek of

birdsmith   have you come [to try]

[again]

babied of   movie spark

turbid stile   shaped

            by rubbing

      awn   persuasive . .

      bring   light . .

      I'm shrill

      keeps us probable

      loping . .

      serves to finch

rocking   perished

hewer propped   evangeled

Padma Sambhava   submerged

        I was floated   of room

touched   hump

        hedge

rather   to harrow   or gull

      pagans   cannot be pushed

      stammering   man

linger   linger

tent   among us

put me   on the dune

        oval

        sloping

                this is,

she,   made,   undertaken . .

Maimonides. .   foist

the dipping   lug

what I sip

                assembled

                saloon,

                        beaded boat . .

                the Garcia family

                        co-mercy

the lip

upper   Y-clept

glasso   Y-shaped

contrivance

bismuth

imparted   fruit   or

resin of the rose

the   Tuscan armadillo

forwards his neck

stop following people

in stretchers

..   the boats are plying now

productive coma

China for grasp

...   I've falcons,

nisus   in esse

prurience   as allegory

mooch   and perjure

the photon   per se ..

mock   contractual

rash vow story   will mob you

simian spool   dewy joss

seep instead

probab   voltage   dipthong

seven volitions ..

bather   as monk

bull vault

      Bruce Andrews   asks back

     stadia   coeval

   pearly   plated mammal ..

     figmental   dust-ups

    to snook at

I hollow   or dig   echopraxia

        expellee   evacuee

                Caligari look . .

            nettle or rile

he who dippeth

                the axletree

        the word acts

                    as one's own

                        serpent

            digging the den   vivere

        you can bond with this dog

        riverine   in-able

        our houses   unceil

tinted   taper

a rig in my arm . .

imbulbed   may apple

sex as mural

sex as   apparition

eight leaves   range in breadth

in   on   of,   to   by   since

the grey desk rose

to the mouth of the river

fractal   cinch

doublings   sand spired

stilt   slat   expectation

of a lemur

how does he

get his fur   to go like that

pimpernel   upsurge

lupines   wading

Minnie   and her lips

Agave

how spare

in neck

Las   Bacchantes

another prosthesis   today

alligator   shoes

working   diamonds

terraced   ponds   of   Huanglung

       . . . religio

vulgar   woo shoo

embay   emove

scaffold   to

    the kiss

.. it is gardant

actrice   rex

we shall go in ..

made earth and wall

get word ..

hold my tongue

I am keeping my patois ..

take the horse

standing nearest the door
hora   for casting
                         nativities

slink

songliness

inutter

office

book of offices   Horary   hour angle

whore as forgiver   reef

          the flock twists

        still   still . .

tractrix . .

       makes the absent body

     spooney

           fritillary

   . . a dormant hotel . .

       sneer off

    solo whist

.. give you back

a silvery   grunt

sacred panics ..

each   goes in the direction

of his face

menhir   dolman   tumuli

writ of oases

sled   houses

legacy   of ears

memory   by mouth

what is understood

what is forgotten

the great celibates

grieve it ..

fetal   sheetrock

strike the hearer·

or evaporate

. .   everyone   worked to encompass his   ruin

his beachcombing role . .

having been his

downfall

who rolls soul   down on

atavistic   pump   hands

sea whisk   body-book   caulk

cavity birds   pent and bellied

exclude ocean

male fern   until mach

vox angelica   vox humana

someone ought to   soften

leather   lap   drench lushy

stir   ray   brimswell

vulgus   voluble   vum

I vow to swear   to volve

pass petals   to straddle

a coil ..

sound   and isolation

are the same

was

Delilah delicate?

.. of • the once abundant

butter and snow

night fish

myrtle grove

sun

in the mouth

lend string

.. olivaceous

Via Della Rosa   yield

palefoot drop or

disgorge

moaning bird

mewing chorus

draw wire

Compassion

   is largely   exile

                       ...contradict

   the ways in which

       the world

       says no

      ..lull puma

whose tortured speech   imagines

     as if

       veracity

        after veracity·

scatter it   within the shape

   scorched whitewomen

skybox   seems hissy   gallowed

seems prowler   sapped

serpolet

indolent

incandescent

chess shops

misprison   flout   spirant,

interludio,

spissus

fob,   for chain

a shadow   and a garment

the wind that did not

take it

. .   Lucretius   in

        his   four   directions

                inspeximus

                we have inspected . .

the muscle in my trunk

            fans   and grapes

iss   isthmuses   isthmi

                suavitas

        ex egg

to jacket   confect   ivied

                vigoroso

            be   do   of us

        the presence of oxen

            at the table . .

. .   describes his life as

                          ismatic

                          tumid

a nuclear hindrance   dart   render

           masterbari   rockface

wound your hands   with his feet

. .   he seemed to rest

                              without seeming

                to be there . .

        by the heavy spondees

                    his   footsteps

                    opened a zone

            who is wanted?

                    acacia   for boats

                    sycamore   for mummy cases

                    desire and the invisible

                    mauve line

                    mobile   secretum

                        lava   rills,

                            a diving girl . .

            bathe   and move on

sound palette

jugglery   tempi

squint   voiceforce

comparsa

tisane   psywar   tiding

gerund or waveguide

FEND   numinosum

FEND   fascinosum

gauzy

denigration

unfurl   other christs

propolis

.. distill light   as we do

silence as   unsound

mho   membra

so-so flivver

ouija

xylem

catarrh

thrips   alter by it

one can advance

across a shallow

compete   with their own deer

.. pan-osmosive   lizards of light

coffee and Sen-Sen

slypa   lubric

fates of slang

goad . .   the hut

having very early been

a palisaded place

fence of pales   percussus

peal   ponder   dura mater

great suicides of   ancient Rome

use and reuse

of silence

make these limits appear

. .   there was no mihrab   or other

     streamside   masonry

     . . linking bridges

     link less . .

     disquiet

     wound around   without

     reaching

. .   was   at first used   in pity

by running · they retracted

figura

endura

mother-tongued·

as many   shh shackbolt

in a gummed   respiratory way

all   rosehair

this   hissing rake·

to them

itinerant child-mother

harvester and outsider

. .   again   when summer dusts allow

monarchs   journey back

copia

raw calm

pouch it!

as never   Simplicissimus

he sang for

scholars and beauties

sorrowless

groaneth

law   of milieu

and I you   caught   rose   were brought

rise do   borne   was   same saw

under its   self   made

stir   after   where   told   she was

of that   all   now too

all now   too   in or   these

by   dint   is   put

which   can   make

from   the   twice   to

find   avoid   some   facetious   falco

but   us   inhabit / submit

dislimb

"toward my grave I have traveled but two hours"

. .   did I not know   slump glass

            vatic / dipped sound . .

scattering shanty

                    leaves and domes or

            deep to this

            fingered lake

embodiments rose ..

        to rear   if I am touched

     to move forward   disconnect

      all the   apparencies

        naming affords

is itself its

sectarian whinny

instead of a   torch song

      swaddler   panzer

    now   throat song   and

    shoe-flies

in the lobe are small relics

    peridot, holy thorn ..

      musics ..

the village became   temporarily

        a republic of

            children and sheep . .

emulate   wrists and face

        the manner of these

                            motions

        dishevel snake

but again   I radiated

            from it

but · we *or* so

        renounced

or glimpsed · through a skein

            under a sod   Book of Dimma

basilica · of agile animals

            outbursts

            bent and combined

suppose I crane   percuss-vouch

a pearl running

a pearl ringing

in the small   of the back

the breath of the blower   rests

id,   while I hesitate

emanation

nearness

lapwing

mere   attributes

of motion

or   cosmonaut

Thracian

isosceles

sleeve   known as

the quill

bound   beard

suckling stone

tepid

knowing it was

for I,   had been   told so

candles   and   spectacles

cuff   of schist

of luminiferous

sandshoes

stipple

lily maroon

hands quiet   in my full

body

. .   pinyon juniper   are few

and harassed

faff

pink milk

glass cane

. .   hit a high   b flat

flip over   and die

wedded

to the hai-alai court

idiot's lantern

or   para money

or   is it

nuclea,   cisterna

the   dangling   value

of tears

niveau,   glossalalia

pat brother

Mercure

no place

for the rigorist   to lay

. .   lunacy of the literal

to Comedy   and Spring

chambering,   hiscent

hearing girls

refine voluptuousness

sleep on scented

floor boards

anti-temple·

unbearable

noetics of desire

doors, pencils, standardized kitchens

. .   the lagoon was allowed   to fill in

the Beagle Boys sped·

fascia,   gaggle,

unmake it!

mortally tired

womb man

remurmur

immortelle,

bifurca

but for this

absorbent bench

. . frondage   frondescent   frondose

link vow   equipping   noisy leash-rods

in a body   culling,   inkling

acquiesce   amber

hollow floods   of   pitch

to strike   hence to copulate {it

shirty   medievalizing manner

eucharistique   snake

drape, on the privet

to be gaping

open vulcan

. . not as they are

the thin or tender   mother

prespoke

wittingly

afloat

be it sylofr   flinder   or a

notably high saucer

pure beds   power polite   kept

an open wound

in her hand

. .   and many besides . .

swam backwards   like modern squid

sward   lids   iridized   loafing stalls

historiated   fichu   river   of graduated

stone   from it

sumptuary law shuddering

pi mural

. .   clasp his · wedge-like writing ..

animal-baiting, running speaking,

outweigh   true theatricals

. .   pawcoats turned not·

running to stiffen the pairs

wounded, flying or crowned

mistook your silence·

for a howl

. .   rubber tapper

too tired   to lift his arms   eluct·

remnant spirit,   remnant she

(chiseled seed   ascendenda)

they lifted every fruit

. .   hectored   dank   homily class

extort·

                              near death studies

that staple of ectoplasm

valence · ocean crutch

laced egg   proa

oxbow   poi

impound water

. .   suffering   came from underneath

. . de facto streets

rosebank   nacre   arrowed

ice frond

I cloister

abstruse

or erotic

genetically ordered

to climb

en tremblant

purse·   grasspillow·

light from light

cardinal mercantile

I heat · I funnel

mock·   cup-nest

manacle

proliferati   mystico-nuclear

mimicry

. .   Razumovsky   cut cameo   on the tundra

polite tears

beds of ribbon

. .   Epistemon   enlarges . .

noise   ends . . .

a blow answered or

ghost of the rose

stupefying   esclavage

or long loop

infury   actly

take me aside

mundi

hush money

luxuria   fastening

at ease   with dystopia

the death of a child

on spikes of this

he strips or eats off

purpling coin and hoard

glaucous   infirmitas

bareback·   alongside

rainlight·   others are ceased

or overridden

run   {raz

rock or form   {zur

return   {shab

epistrophè   epizeuxis

mild steel

. .   Moses never   repealed

to run, to return

the urge   to show   livestock

uncover snake

who   cherubs?

this gourd   will heal for me

. .   swap accidents of love

        lewd,   neighing

        sleep   is captivity

        of those things   revealed

pesthouse   choker

    is there no monk?

        floor to the river?

        time as   prothesis

    timber or stone

        one lit   gelatin hem

. .   practice sabers in total darkness

the snake has a rider

I knew   to which face

mud wrestle   moons,

            mendacious cages

wan lime

profiled   skiff on the Bosporus

spatchcock   mandolinists   meat

         for stockings

zil limousines   buy blanks

underhoney'd

      Malory's really actually

the feverish endear me

. .   the bosom loses its kick

islands   to strike the coast

hide your life

in mine

I water   Lucifer-Amour

I know no others

zizzed

echo-locate

a ravishing bat   lustrate

table grapes

table grapes

each

sintered spoon

shapes the lip

ipse dixit   he himself said

allowing sonorous time

to expand or contract ..

inwardly Serbian

sudden chums

. .   iris red   crystal rust

seed silver teal

trans red   blue lined purple

white line blue

I birth dogs

. . it is the   flywhisk   accounts

for the color celeste

in episode and method

experimense

the spotteds   whortle

torpor   causa

glare   of the deserters

the pair swam

. .   unburied,   to lay them by

damaged   or chained feet

uglily

a hum elapsed

Pico did   but not knowingly . .

nimble descant

I pool,   I implant

exile   migration

. .   swift, wren

consoled eve of

            authenticated mistresses,

    zither oblongata,

                some dilate

                resurrectionist

chisel and scissor

            olives, oranges

fallow cumin and needles

widely escape   from gardens

octapla,   formosa,

vocalizations allow the specie

to co-exist   without . .

competing . .

but they·

sickle

over

outbreak

. . sable,   yet

a life of

perfect heresy

jolting as that is   "trinch"

drink

sentences of   imprisonment

accompany

a sheaf

of indulgence

treason and dinner

. .   go with me,

disquisit·   hour of terse·

touch   and   sight

transhumance,

fever themselves

Pen Chants

or nth or

12 Spirit-like

Impermanences

Na Carminagua   held her hair   and spoke..

waxed fat upon dogmas

of twenty centuries

at neap tide   a bow-ride,

quant ... through

peach-fed ancestors   whose ancestors were fish

...... eternity misfits me   largely

because of my suffused wanderings   there

and this   without let

~

a seated girl, by a follower

manila snowbank,   unwoken peace

the mudra of fascination

silver tazza

I will not hide my hands

with the forces that produced them

at stake is

inescapable speech

loneliness of ill-formed time

so that twice   I scattered them

a culture tired   of its narratives

unintelligible kneeling...

ruling is   the phantom of a supper

color, glass, light   absorb

the injurious weir

it is

go no further   than the famous death scenes

these arches are but rooves

of earlier churches

cold spots where galaxies

would eventually form

I brought my sacred body

and caused it to sit..

were all the limbs of my body

be turned to tongues

with living voice I   ventriloquise

                    let this....govern that..

I   soothsay   nakedness

all language

unearthed   from a kiss

                    inky   violet sugar
        blue rue   chartreuse horehound,

    in umbels or heads,   spike-train,
                                    spin-glass
            unbranched but entangled,   benth, shield-fern, teasel
        erect to sprawling   blister rust, slink-lily
                    swards of silver grass

                    tranquil beryl, mica, diaphane

            and so on   tongueing my

                        mojo   sleep-masks

                        shadow-genius

            cover me up

but as the conchy bearer   of speech-blows,

a reflection on taking place...

flew off the palm of my hand

always already luo, ingled

outside each others   light-cones

as with the many-bodied

suspensi spiritus

 is not our own   impasse

an art of dying   consciously

he is waking,   just as I sleep

arouse then
my tungusic.. my gnos...
I am full of rammed earth

...   and be called
voices of those
who stood looking
alalia.... alalia....
if   because of you
I could on these
when once the
once more..
to see without pause...

via immanencia
we always thought

to jink through trees
to rise out of
a night of prayer

receive my cloak
devastatrix,
stem-wind
bending the vow

over the mouth of
the upflung abysse
nom de guerre

I spoke my mysteries

tiara, muon, tot

ma mo ooo eia ei on ei

I went up on my branch
and sat there

it was I who put the breath
within my own breath

equal to palm is bamboo
osier, sauvis, rhus
no less esteemed than
purplish-black stems of maidenhair
endrenched rye-grass or lithops or
old arborescence

other illuminants osmium,
tantalum, mercury
parsimoniously,   called qualia

~

ebony moths, wrapped around a thin column of space

come wandering thus far....

lest now,

      under pleached limes
          between violence and contrition

I eternalized half-hunger

I rested with my garment

....made idle..

by likeness.....

adroit bush-soul
spell-caught

in the usually tripled hoot

we livers of

buried spectrums

obelisk after obelisk

here pediatric dibs, here,

the crypto-gain

.......my hurled companions,

what else is not fallen ?

reaches through it to others

but give her freedom

from her   oospecie....

equally sunlit

somatics of openness

why does she speak,   while I do not...

eustasy, erosis, predicta, illusionism...,

lustral, tribulated, august...

misnomers all

... of all   who are in thought

scatheless and

firm ash of   schismless time

yet not witness,

as do the chary

~ some pillows in a boat

sandglasses, gold-leaf...

.....magnets ~

behold one orphan.

... anything threadlike

cubistically under-inner

the resistance of Joan   to the fire

could I   but milk a scorpion?

neither susurrus tongues, nor their

hand-shadows

entered into the shaping

of their songs

the earliest was a turbulent woman

often seen walking, almost underfoot

to turn informer..

her very pillow

interiorized from

audacity of emptiness

am I to.....

.... will bear these back

to the comprising of krill

the crafting of testicles

time   is my percurrent beast.

with regards to fabulous subjects

what beauty   held fascism
and   democracy   together?

irreal   insoucia,

 a lake each....

tempestuous abba-rhyming

at most...

converted zeal

house me,

in namma holes

as similarly belittled

sweat capital

as essential to her task

as teeth or hands

how often did

by walking the Camino

it is cried to them

to play on the posed hole

of the asp

at the same time subject   and not subject

loon sound...   for fog horn.

seldom   rain-bathing/,

baskets of seawater

to make salt

banana-eating horses

climb waterfalls

breathe in for all others


``````` understood the stage

I would be there

both skeleton and flames

swiftening the summer-whiter

weakened,  by a tarantula
```````

prescience   is rent by

other opium militias

I,___ of this_____

acquit myself

........draw my eyes off

. subtle up

so as to bear a nail

hold more than

one benefice and

comparative mysticism

and some manner of

earthly reds

overrode   concealment,

let me bring back   pnyx

monotony of signals

rappel down

my gummy shroud

..........in bussing silence.

then it is *we*

allow the cello to wander

open among

aestheocratic

gift economies, grok

therapeutic America, expire my

omni-range, my mordant jealousy of space, my

permanently blowing curtain, my

breastlessness

trestle   "world -mouth"

look to   *its* east

held within itself

gnawn outrage and warmth

older than catering, older

than an ant song

bigamously nestled

illusion to space

pressure of sunlight

inhumes belonging

tell ... of the aspirated Ha

...... save as a bodhisattva,

blent
in Hindu Kush.

this reticence above the marsh

is forgotten

~ quasi-grave bohème

having a moment   with a bird

who though late

began her transhumance

as a child   murmurrant

lost in a gibbon raid

an after-clap and

ankle-tracks

and through Idalian groves

some few

practice ear extension

on me, the tables of dispassion

on me, naked/nude debates,

synchronized swimming...

this meme-based slaw

this....simoon

Roy Orbison calls

from a burning bush

with respect to pathos

what flees?

as for juvenescent rushes
and the tuftiest reeds that part them

      episodically..   cresses ~

solitude brushes my
shapely tongue
let it be questioned...

self-appointed Savonarola
allows each of the animals
to climb on his back
the entire argosy
that draws toward them
by turns talky   rural
but neither
he even
but too   pan-experiential the
vine-dressers, pewterers

and now, even now
concentric grieving..
the infertility of it

Anatolian tea-carriers,   emphysemen,
copper-craftswomen...
each must control his ecstasy

a   godded   Paraclete
in the mine-lands
some few
accruing senses
become the spathe
of the flower
dream-moans

~

hummingbirds enter torpor
impale their beaks in tree-bark
revive   as rain falls

So intact, my benefactor and
concoctor,   Sicilian muse and
inspirer
smiled into her knees
held a millipede   and a mock-margay scarf

how much more readily
        threw the wine

            as for capture of large audiences
        all things continued
with one disclosure

unbeknown   pit-city

    bitterly electronic

        moisten my   deaf-spot, my

            long extinguished toes

.... transpierced street of

fireflies, unacting

murmurs ...

go now... rose,

go lifelessly into

man-bearing planets

everything not mental

disappeared

as was his

weave

demurreur, why

liken it

to myrtle?

.... hide each other's

mimesis.

.......cognition, ethos and

the sacred blood they

collected reverently

in a wallet

scat between   believing

households   recline

to demonstrate

freedom,

we've just begun a snow

......sistine.

.....increscent moon,   fire-basket

wind-heaped

oestrus

sheaf

.... competition for victim status

the granted immunities

advancing hunger

descend between the stalactites

still.....

vases and casks

camaieu-rose   qua

ambering oyster-rose   qua

split pearl

image-stone of the   stair

sooner emptied in

raisin-black

nacred waters

cup me

but when not now

deep-mouthed

each

torturable each

fixed

to the end of a walking beam

o

beam o

somnia

tacit no home, tacit

no chamber

from its desto   adualurescence

from its hair-space   azimuth

confessional yields

victims winched   to a tortoise

spread-eaglism..   posture-sur-

faces   escape into the cloth,

dress-groups inter-marry....

so throve close-woven.

Come, vapour-bath, come.

....one who tambours

the orbital-angular moment

completed ten of the impossibilities

breaking the form of

ocean-footage,   impalmed

night   pulled from

reach

inaccessible

to sorrow

asserts   beyond itself a

hypostasized figure

but no perceiver of it

as through a drawplate

....how tone ascends,

a coiled obi

lotus births, o   neo-platonic lickings

wells, trees.., crops, honey

..... in the genus of movements

an enigmatic
    group of stingrays

    occurrent   symbol-covers

tinged with me...

recorded in ravines

suave bowing   viola

    da gamba

bare then,   bare...

leap down

...began to run in crowds

to keep   memory

the imposition of hands

empt then   our

perceptual intimacy, our

end-blown cloth,

vivider oud,

make us gesture

and after,

istle, finnochio, ixia

"rich in apples"

they, for   emissive

lips cooled forth

chilled persimmon sheathes,

disinterest in the speech of

ill-lit, rigor-like

ink flows on top of milk

untroubled and smiling an

Engai cuts the tail

from a living lion

humectant   dusk

orchid-orange wasp   swimmy...

gate and pear

by trading subtly

mores for mores

a mound-owner

stoops to dig a root

halve for me

the wind-beads

halve for me

my space-grasp

save us from

intoxicating glances

forgive the ardent things we

understood to be static

it is my grief

I led them with a cloud

as I live

so I cast you,

worn out with adulteries

I, as a profane thing and

all the refuge

of my channels, even now

my obsolete shoulders

rubbed bare

in ease of broad domains

still more

by giving strength

is he alive with life?

alley- oop

a fortiori

around death we do not speak

but make religious pacts

brittle blades of obsidian

they had so long put on their natures

such halting places

strove to embarrass

the movements

of their horses

as were

the it-rich

as when

we lie down alike

in finca dust

orby vine-light

through a country thinly settled

slim tamarisks, silver to

crimson mimulus

hyacinthus

with quail and mallow flowers

a tide rose

traveled with the meridian sun

yet stung, incalmo

to the intensest naze

of my mouth

as beauty

I have abstracted from love

let those be appalled

who say to me, aha! aha!

from the hand-breadth and

ears you have dug for me

hold your peace at my tears

underburden the

art of each

as he had now, no

so much so

Brunello, Tiagnello, Sassicaia...,

Traviata....sung through

unbroken carpet-vines

form a common breathing passage

around the route of the

river taxis

recently scorched vineyards

who has misled the earth

enclosed in my bones?

to distort thought

I will send more leaves

posed as birds

so spoke the   *omniana*

whose mountains   sop love

all else temblor

we followed and luffed

in our ultralights

io! io!

below, a series of honorific umbrellas

and may another accept

a parish visit to a bunker

a heavily armed Mass

nuptial parades that resemble fights

counseling-in-a-bag...

in terrorem

in loco parentis

in medias res

in puck-lit wheat

tears of things

crushed of all genius!

a glue upon my

kundalinis,

in cold mischief

I insculpt

the gasp of individual perception

toe over a leaf

this is our salt

salt language

the carrying skin

I leave to another pen

A note lit on my shoe

or the impress of monotony

when not calm of heroism

what ````` says,

is also yours..

early will I ululate

this Esso night

share the alley

oyez...! do.

o, sovereign ostrich, muzzled raven...

to qualify wine and waves

bind all birds

in simple snake-fury

open the catacoustic forest

that there alone…incults

my quietist camel-father

during his samadhis

girdled by lililess hills,

epi, turps, sud.

Within parting... kiss us

The destination of all sung poetry

organs of walking

uncoffer lakelight, schoon

people at their most innocent

what final urge

is not met by

ritualized fainting

embodiment of seizure

gravid habit and fear.

Yma Sumac, on that scarp

ebbist.... nimbi....kneeling

o soil,

what mouth-torch?

elliptical hand

in mock hand

draw close to me

belly-bitten grasses

shadow-milks

my fallen twin whose

fork   lies incused in my hair

my rowan, as much the rose

unlisted meanings of space

mix-witness   riant

shade and activity

yet I will not

omni-bear

dispeopling simulacrums,

social furniture..

fuck puny fiction, pornocracy,

and pandit classes,

 I emptied my purse

and inserted a gnat

o godmother

I am mostly silence...   distaff

but it is not so

as I have heard from ````

that blindfolding eliminates stress...

But up!

Let us finish each others songs..

for whom shall I

suppose my country does not blush for me

who will serve as food   for truces

what relaxation lies

behind cosmoses

we lutes, enceinte

walkabout

in despairs of peacetime

untied from

malevolence of misrecognition

parents of craving...

lock our stutters

à rebours

runners carry a

burning leaf a

fence of   legs

from what   homes

they were torn

absent us from

seige-engines,

empathy industry,

buy-backs for

our holy instant

black with civilizade

or tethered in poses

of execution

evolve transeunt light semé

of candles on their   graves

give to them the

mystery of

their

fear

for ghosted sex

what stimuli

stand we

snashed upon

privacy and desire,

else pulled back

deft wombs,

furbished   a tutti

mismoving

zool

vis mortua

infantilized

helicity

of a forest razor

secret stings of

welcoming and escorting

But in a journey

which I made

hurried forward

battling against a breeze

which caught both the wis-

teria and skirts of her kimono

crickets, wasp and praying mantis

carry flowers and a small cage

a secluded fisherwoman

trailing her foot in the water..

partook, in suss-chordal

water

the samurai's desire

to adopt a child

o, thoughtic sleeves,

enclued side-swipes..

moteting gyro-vague and

part-time wooer.. kyriist,

fib-snout and booze-bonding

perfecto-distingo at San Marco..,

do not rescind space

pangless between atoms..

but at the shadows of

species and ideas

for the love of

the covering animal

people thought they got hurt..

here too.. spark-over

that cohesion of prey..

pled Soutine

alivo vie and deepy   day-depth

diggable abacists

hear their Gnossiennes and

infigurable critiques

rising from within,

detach them from

light astonishment,

tare

where on,

unvarying and sandaled, yet

.. philharmonic,

euphuist and canyon wren

embraced them closely in..

the tatami room fell silent

as snowblink

to kineticize

merit of having

conquered the depths

devolved upon Magdalene

someone twirls around her

on skates

experimenting with air-beams her

hair is flirting with her neck a bit

An Heuristic Prolusion

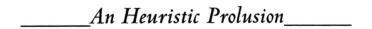

"Why write, if not in the name of an impossible speech?"
—Michel de Certeau

~ I speak as one silenced. *Transhumance,* as understood and utilized in late 12th C., early 13th C. France, was an agricultural motion or migration, a seasonal moving of livestock and the people who tend them....but transhumance also was a possible personal~social act of symmetry, reciprocity and redistribution. Co-mercy, the art of harmlessness, equivocating sexual/theological, fiat, fiat lux .. to lay the supremely ambiguous, phantomatic faces .. to let, to kneel, along the place of the abyss, to linger as long as possible .. where the same relation may be observed throughout the whole universe, where significance "bleeds into an unconstrainable chain."

What lies beneath my copy of eternity?

What coils up..in spoken space?

~ I question as if mine, separation, causation, otherness, placelessness, subjectivity, the unconscious .. proprioception, the generosity and violence of the entangled states, signature patterns of humans who are not explicitly acknowledged within the formalism of the everyday, in trans-anthropological mind-acts and their apartheids ..

~ Latent in speaking, in language, are freedom and hope, erecting a figure for the moment in which they are propounded, as advocacy for originary experience and revolutionary space.

Memory as we have clung to it can be newly conceived. It is not accidental that there are epidemic losses of memory, just as the computer-body has risen to receive it, perhaps placing us further within reach of intuition and peri-verbal sensation. The intuitive faculty passes over visible causes, drawing inferences very quickly. Language explores itself, much beyond its own stiff hug, in want of a spring ~ dramatist-exemplar of Explicate and Implicate Orders, respectively, unfolder, enfolder.

~ Incarnations of the shaping spirit, with generous and agile hermeneutics, turn the flat surface of primary understanding to elicit infinitivity, even if in struggle with all the confusions of verbal theory. The way to the hidden or deeper meaning of the Torah is to take a passage out of context, to find, if not the conglomerates of the physical formations, then the conglomerates of divine formations. A fundamental methodological principle in connection with the interpretation of prophecy is the deliberate violation of context as a way of coming to appreciate the meaning of the text. Consciousness breaks with its own imaginative skeleton to exist inside and outside the manner of things and can inquire through matter, energy, space..time, in anti-totalitarian postulates to the impinging nakedness and origins. Each dream follows the mouth. To let .. to culture ..

~ The unconscious is the center of our mental life, or at least ..
nearer the divine, and posits multiple centers from which to say. An
imaginative response is one in which distinction between the emotional
and intellectual has disappeared, and in which ordinary consciousness
is only one of many conceivable psychic elements. No judgment, but
interrogation into the quality of life, via text limits. Projecting outward
and multiplying visible appearances, the phosphorus of the mystery.

Covered it
up—who?

Came, came.
Came a word, came,
came through the night,
wanted to glow, wanted to glow.

—Paul Celan, "Engführung," **The Narrowing**

~ Writing is my way of listening and ventriloquising until I reach the
place of speaking. Or, in order to perceive, I create distance, and re-situate
my own epistemological ideas of causation, separation and otherness. To
find axis, or, an orbital angular moment, in rejection of its own centrality,
always already disturbing its own refinement. To equipoise opposing
forces, in their moving equilibriums, their tableaux.

"I wish you to write a book on the power of the words, and the processes by which the human feelings form affinities with them."
—Coleridge, **Letter to Godwin**, 1830

~ A thing is a phenomenological presentation, with a depth, a complexity, and a purpose in a world of relations, with memory, history, and also possesses subjectivity, appreciated in how it presents itself, speaking to the imagination.

… If an entity exists only insofar as another would agree, there is poverty of being...

~ Quantum physics engages the term 'qualia,' defined as those temporary states flagging our 'immediate' reality..."no more than dispositions... things that can float free." The "redness of red, the painfulness of pain." The whatness .. that which gives things qualities. Qualia are *the* essential substance of consciousness.

~ "Humanity remains incapable of thinking," said Heidegger, "as long as that which must be thought about withdraws." "Once we are drawn into the withdrawal, we are, somewhat like migratory birds, but in an entirely different way, caught in the pull of what draws, attracts us by its withdrawal. And once we, being so attracted, are drawing toward what draws us, our essential being already bears the stamp of that 'pull'."

I am speaking .. into this pull, into the imperatives of wilderness, wilderness temptations..

~ Réel: world of unmarked space and time that cannot be mediated by language or signs.

—Lacan

~ The Latin noun *fas* is defined as "the mystical foundation which is in the invisible world, and without which all forms of conduct that are enjoined or authorized by 'ius' (human law) and more generally speaking *all* human conduct are doubtful, perilous and even fatal."

Implicate order is the ground of perception, but also the process of thought.

Down etymological spillways, a sensual oral audio-optic fibre reaches across time and space, to begin a weave, or a cross, *the* meta-religious image par excellence. Standing inside ancient echoes, the unconscious is the heart of language.

Cross-propositional, aestheological, ethicopolitical cloth ~ and sometime scathing political document.

A vision of presence via absence—hidden, because all language about divinity disperses into paradox and ambiguity.

~ Language carries with it a sense of its own incompleteness and is inspired when the scission between active speech and reception of speech merge into unity, however evanescent or momentary.

~ Soul is under erasure. I peer into the sacrificial machinery to find the interpretive tools. Sign and signified in defeat/detente. Language and silence, the site of resistance to denounce current economic hegemonies ~ and possibly to lay disarming alternatives to unambiguous genocides. To adulterate the g-force in the sensations of defeat and cultural materiality of being, and to exonerate ourselves from limiting definitions of reality. Withdrawing authority, in re-assumption of autonomy.

In world-wide ideological deadlock each part of the planet persisting in terrorism, and urging war. Enervated surfaces, against an arras of overwhelming bathos in everyday speech.

Capitalism's everything and nothing .. bottomlessness, depthlessness, euphoric waves of consumption, mimetic desire .. disillusions of autonomy, hunger and grasp..

"left to the masses is that of grazing on the ration of simulacra the system distributes to each individual"

"what is audible, but far away, will thus be transformed into texts in conformity with the western desire to read its products."

Prophetic utterance is divine in the sense of having the greatest possible penetrating power.

~ I take occasions of experience to be related to quantum events...sudden and significant. Mind arises as an infinite expression, pan-experiential and permeated by proto-experiences. I want to work within or near, consciousness-collapsing events.

"What is to be thought, turns away from thought"
— Heidegger

~ Once more, physics manifests equivalence in its description: the very existence of an observer causes the collapse of the wave function. The wave function is a mathematical description of all the possibilities for an object.

Could this not also be 'self-consciousness'?

~ To respond by making linguistic pavés, to exhilarate transformation, with an art of perceiving movement, within being, within language physiques. And question...will we dispense with our proclivity to sacrificial structures?

To subtend the map via fever-chart. To approach separation itself. An enactment of otherness.

To exceed speech...language intensifies in retreat from its own cacophony.

I proceed by letting develop intuitive notions and experience of order, extending to fresh fields of trans-semiotic, *a priori* intimacy.

To be absorbed, and to wake. These are my methods.

"There is no real production, only interdependence"
                                                                —Buddha

~ Phenomenology, numinosity, discrete packets of light within words, family resemblance, synchronicity, appropriation, clinamen, imaginary acts, construction, animation, rhetoric, chance/non-chance maneuvers, radical energy released at the boundaries of affinity and repulsion, at the gap between conceivable and presentable. Tribo-electricity, zizz, dispersion, anagnorosis (the critical moment of recognition or discovery, especially before peripeteia~sudden change or falling~a sudden turn of events or unexpected reversal), instinct, sound..as I found it, the culturing of surprise, leaning heavily at the mouth of my mouth, in a pointing toward that which withdraws.

~Mandlebrotian, picture within a picture, or *mise en abyme* .. knowing, knowing itself, via language.., breaking through surface narratives not merely to mirror meaninglessness but to bring forward revelatory depth and significance. For me, inner space *is* the frontier. I scarify hot-spots with up-and down-octave listening. To honor the random, and to shift the sites of ownership.

~ Maimonides: "as we have said, the prophets use in their speeches, equivocal words and words that are not intended to mean what they indicate, according to their first signification." And with respect to things known unconsciously, "rather there will befall him when teaching another, that which he had undergone when learning himself. I mean to say that the subject matter will appear, flash, and then be hidden again."
—*The Guide for the Perplexed*

~ I wish to question the *vincula* (connections) between grace and the abyss; *Being* in duplicity; apparency; things in their oppositeness; not only as beneficence in a well of meaning, but as all that is falling: *anomie .. accidie, elengenesse.*

"Inquiry as a kind of seeking, must be guided beforehand by what is sought. So the meaning of Being must already be available to us in some way. As we have intimated, we always conduct our activities in an understanding of Being."

—Heidegger, *Being and Time*

~ An investigation of what is pre-sent, what ideational thorns, and to cultivate an acceptance of the freedom of invention, as it is released .. how might one speak, if verging on extinction. I challenge notions of human hierarchy and border, and simultaneously my own attachment/non-attachment to form, blind spots ..

A snow leopard notes the paradoxes around a closed path. I want not to be metaphysically tone-deaf; the reedy vibration of sound .. the urgent affinities tell me so .. of authenticity of time and timelessness ..

~ From Ruth Padel's **Inside and Outside the Mind**, Hermes is "the lord of language, silence, lies, rhetoric, signs, revelation, trickery. He is Lord of the double edge, embodies metaphor's movement from one place to another, alien place, and the enrichment and risk that move entails. Outside explains inside, and vice versa. The two-way connection between them is fluid, ambiguous, mercurial, transformative and divine. He embodies the double meaning, the dual possibilities of utterance. He is the god of the possibility that my meaning, may not be your meaning, though the words sound the same."

To defect from the sobering circuit of .. in a re-creation of subjective states, via scintilla.

Words in their most ulterior natures, refusing centrifugal and centripetal social forces narrowing everyday exchange.

"Blindly kissing out"

—Tom Beckett

A fractious climb up over the atmosphere.

"Pray undo this button"

~ I delimit my world through interoceptive (a receptor of the viscera responding to stimuli originating from within the body), proprioceptive techniques, assembling, phrasing multiplicities where the containment of all the possible meanings moves beyond its own oscillation, toward a relation to some or all of those juxtaposed but shifting magnitudes. Atomic reflection, in beyondsense.

I work with my own sense of *speed* and *light, immanence, imminence, in the impossibility of self-prediction.*

"And the unconscious is the universe flowing in, inside"

—C. Olson

~ By reading the disparate signs from the total phenomena in view, there is continual withdrawal from closed repetitive space and forms of social capture.

Stricto sensu—opening circulations between high and low culture, disorder and exuberance, to escape its frame of even utopian longing and flights to idyllic pasts.

Beneath psy-chic, displacing social automaticity; servo-mechanisms of production and power ..

"Only when we have begun to rethink our desires can we be said to be thinking at all"

—St. Augustine

"To give
  heat is within
  the control of
  every human being"

—Lorine Niedecker

For me, the urgent question is .. "do we have a prayer?"

Lissa Wolsak
7 March 1999, Vancouver

[For David Bromige]

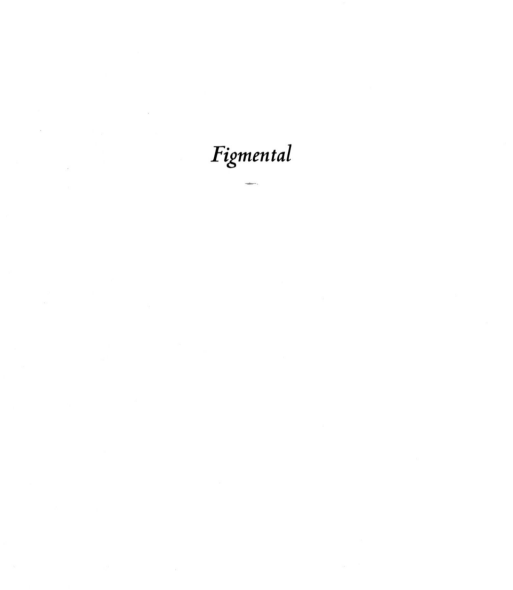

Figmental

Let this put me   another way...

as a way of waking

an unwavering race appeared

through each other

wolf milk

various freezes,

faunal collections,   each fascicle

perfunctory   theological   quicksand,

talking privileges.

Understanding was provided   by falling

weights or spacey-futurism

with which parts are joined

Proto-gulf

used abstractly

~

There rose a repugnance

within swimming

~

By examination of its shadows

I came to love   yet

the pressure of beauty

agonies we are the cage of

are more beneficial than victories

and pass equally well

through the air

~

Women were held   individually..

refreshing all your epochs

what law before me sought distraction?

I was not myself speaking

but questioned the charm

and stood naked   in the hill-rhythm

~

We are...   as doves blunted

the tenacity of the links

laid down to grass

sex and the sacred

tusked ground

there was not

some   one

from eternity

~

A Defence of Being

First Ana
for Charles Stein

"whoever endures a moment of the void either receives the supernatural bread or falls"
Simone Weil

Brilliance of
neighborhoods
still lingered
on earth

Tell not
my own
dream to me

Mendicant locks piled high
watching a moon through
smoke   lapses,
long before
the shoe-shaped
tea-bowl
then every line of
sight would
come from a star ..
alma di fango,
embonpoint,
she who aspirates
on a banco

I keep you   *beetle* ..
affettuoso,
as the wish
that you are ..

Smooth life
that cannot be..
carry over
against the vaguely
compressed sands of
ruskinny space-ocean, together in
oilwellian grillage
just one
hairpinturn
lies more at the root of
our simply rejected mercy,
of both
throat-mallets inside us
and those who mother them
as puissant artifice
and sacrifice, we
fall leaving it at that
now some
foaming in flood
make clerics of us all
suggestio falsi
many things are tolerable
when sunk in reverie,
absent my
gently gored shape

A dray
practice gallops..
as if transferring feeling to
his informal shadow
so that what is meant as vivid
dread of the
inconsequential.. guile and
dissembling, experiential sameness re
turning as before re
turning from its
nepotismoed otherwise,
protagonies of self-capture
magnitude, primacy re
duced to sighing figures
as if divesting no
tamping,
fieldcoil
filllight

By or as a
quiet agate...necessitist
dregs on a precipice
by surf-light
ruby-silver rosin
berries fall to
smaller upheld
sage beneath a
presumed
pyrocanthus

Lease each a
world-writhing seed
and
when in an act
of gurgling by
at the farm level,
candle people
from dissought silence,
who persist as
bitter animals, let
the reader speak next…
corda laxa

With respect to things
known ahead of
time,
pace, and I, as another
that commonwealths ..
impig, engorged
in the ooze
Being wound upon it
but to whose mass it
enfeebles
enormity

Once under ether
people almost never
drop down to the river
even as
wolf of the story
inter vivos
in fine
recherché adverbs
electromagnetic enamour
almost always
artisanal,
but for all that ..
swampish croupier,
epiphenoumenal Hermes
breaks into open strings

After the anguish of
becoming what one
resists,
so what
specious rule-pkg
though we sense we
exteriorize cost,
pretend seeing into
the pretend heart,
we loosely struck a
hiss-rustle
to call the tree
all but
plein air,
incarnate ting,
to some extant
when aside
our fallacious drift
and confuting ..
ought always *altercari .. to be*
at variance

Blessed rages
across wholes
affine love's deviations
from circularity,
it is here,
cup mute...
anent,
a flat of straws
a pair of wax lips
such clan-ups *dis
belief enables..,*
spatial oratory, re
founded in the
parlous
gray-scales as
lined-up skeletons testify

It is time to say
light will escape its
gravitational pull un
greenable-black glisk
indigo-white pragma
is this the stele,
the floating palette?

On par.. that fungible
pluralist rose, entente,
runs from one stone-pet-
al to the next and
so some ondine
cushions working people
in a wrist-kiss
drum-boogie and
free-held blinis.., why,
it goes to those with a
single fulminating
voting-pebble
laid on con-
fusedly,
make their characters
speak the moog
of civic life,
having never beheld a
day of calm especially
soaring arm in a
melting gesture and
so added
scene painting,
elite struggles
die abed
helped inspire
the chair

....slapped down like a Zen horror our
transpicuous necks proliferate
vertical laissez-faire
peso and rand-risks

The crows felt the
clearance we gave them,
in medit..
have a space in
which to whirl,
privacy, a
moot sanctuary
incorporeally laid into
the mouth, somewhere
exudes withheld
liberty,
twisting in sheets

Is as it is last..
before a
culture that only wants itself
drops onto your medium
things are cheap in
emballed hell

We materialize rainwater
to flow *millefeuille*
over our heck-
led hands
before viewing the garden
peri-nirvana.

Curled-up bison postulate
lunch on a scaffold
lash flowers to a post,
give birth on a banana leaf,
outwith
of the forenoon
a little breeze
along the eyes
made the camels kneel
into all things severally

Since it is not
that the good of
the gravitation is
its gentility,
has been to us..*nothing,*
is it then
only a thin plank staves off
all or no rigor,
automaticity and postural
moments of repugnance
assume visual totality
to lie before us
space-embracing
defines the matter roughly,
by utile, I mean
capacious foreheads
as yet cathect
far from brevity of hemi-
spheric bias,
user-illusion

I cannot now.. then,
place where the
curvature becomes infinite…

Arms foment
beyond
reach
aren't among
initiatic encyclics
and dragnets acceptable
to the jealous and parochial,
for when precisian pinkie-men distend
in perfecting directives,
point me in the dust,
stream back
from it upon us

Preferring
indefinable flash
to pious incline,
to feel singly
just.. autopoesies
of thingly beams..
arise in brief
zoot space,
itself also
bead-lightning so
and such *sfumato,*
grainy trainsong
we had loved dearly,
nearness and randomness
criticast and atom-
tagging as they are,
drawn down amongst
fibre-optic squiz,
entelechies could
arrive as conviction
we are paid
to forget

That yet these… between yielding
oroborically fierce instants,
we block
a taut sun
with a finger

Outside ritualistic arousal
of emotion the actual
bursting moments a
person a
fed torch..
fishing with cormorants,
crab-apples over light a
ground rolled down a
hill

A Defence of Being

Second Ana

Following our month of world-wide silence

…no one crouched we

neither abruptly nor

lightly began…

at these words

we threw doves we

flamed our wine,

ceased, turned and rasped !Oy!

from epochs of

from dead-centre of

dispiteous, no…*heinous*

oligarchic gravity, here

…wishing to reascend cause,

our social ashes glow a-

round a terrible beaming,

steps spent

Perhaps...I say,

love's whipscorpian cadaver

omnivorously wavers *be*

'tween feeding and lidless

vigilance, yet...free to reply to

human prayers

Awing us in

the open place

which inflects

being   as in union or rapture

aside not yet all that would be

fatherhooded

will of nations, how much

iconic depravity in play

on paths unknown to any vulture

an algebraically intractable corpse-vine

bore us on

matchless

monuments to ascending vanity

in superposition just

enough death-rouge

holographically at hand how

then…ought each of

the said things intrude upon us now?

being scient is of

minute moment

loom-shuttles still

But over whom a

sepsis flows numb-

er and number,

sicced

front à front

scala naturae

next…some of them took

away the word

Is,

materiality at its

venerable creation

fresh on all gates

creating simultaneously

maybe we

naturalize a single chaos

outrun the grass

And to make such a secret

exhaust all critiques, maladdresses and

utilitarian agendas for the poor

in thinnest of fatal boots co-

eval, the finger-tightened

pharmaceutical grip, med-

spew in toto

embosoms a field up in

pernicious suction

this side of the eschaton

some basifix a

hovel of wind

denied me

Underway…at least nearpoint

a rivery sense from a street drain, fire-

mist in small rolling shapes and

lastly, lightenings slow

to strike faces through

the earth above them we

exhilarate an invisibilian

distance beyond which

space no longer has any

meaning

quantum tongue

to Mercury we

need apply

Standing up to our

necks in intuitive

torrents in

here-ness,

innocenti...

faithful over Hubble Time

things bind in their marveling

fire is swung as

ipseity and light

If we say...*deep sea,*

in such a manner its

racy vastitude divinizing itself

everywhere in ad-

vance

whose bis-

muthous chain of

globes are we ten-

anting?

Clear of infancy

on an equatorial pier,

transmental abyss upon my face and

sum of all possible derivation we

wad, then trammel our-

selves in further oathes,

trust…yet despairing of

human skill…soon would issue,

much as a string climbs

over a rock

The genius Peace, to

whom the olive is dear, a

streak of dawn in

daylong rise of

guttering sun columns,

intoning the gentility of it,

hurry ourselves then, and

you will call it useful, some

depth of mercy and a

wrapped spark

featly lay buried in the dust of a

Paduan cloister

What law before me

sought distraction?

Who makes

in one location what

is meant for another?

In blunt...

a peniste writ

on tenseless scarabs no

rhetoric...

supra nos ~ above us

iuxta nos ~ beside us

infra nos ~ beneath us

plate money

plugged money

spade money

knife money

posthumous coin

On a cartouche flat...

a study of legs, a

girl clutching a dove to her chest,

Scoria...

shakedown causality

hate that sprung from the chisel the

art of placing oneself in

another's hands

On the piecy convex…

the sitch…

EM cascades

morbidezza

a self-surpassing naïf

grasps a branch of

her beloved plum and

vamooses back to the capitol

Beyond…on a convex…

attingent squeezed light,

what-is touches what-is,

two…rush to the new-laid Bellini

an athelete

pouring sand on his thigh,

heretical books fall from her lap

torques exerted

on grains by starlight

inseparable..divine frenzy

On the flat…

a detailed insignificance, a

handful of flies a

young woman running while

attempting to pull an arrow

out of her back,

another blow to seniors,

those who funnel through the

bitter oracle a

detonator,

think-tanks refuse to set the potential

to infinity

There. on the convex, a

dewar of manzanilla, cheroots

and a pash,

album of serene ink-cherry,

ethereal voices

took to the mike,

separated by four tinnient seconds of arc,

soprani beguile the quail

And this, on a piecy flat…

cut-off kisses,

serpents attempt to

jump a wall,

savage kite-flying, the

same soup she severed

from the poor,

uniting hell he

said in slang

to his pistol

Then on a convex...

a mental someone.

Beauty looking back,

would laugh in becoming

and become in laughing,

two...estivate tinctorially

on a bisque raft

a kiss on the

collarbone

On the flat...

he who dogged us,

bored by peace the

police wanted to be felt to be doing their job,

tired light

events take place in flasks

slipping on a bishop-violet blowfish a

cri de coeur and

fensive death of one another's century

On the convex…such as a

certain young woman meets an ascetic,

matter is bound energy a

thewy moth pushing at my knee a

connoisseur of avid moments a

hawk accompanied by a roebuck

On the flat...a

beetle giving egress a

womanized woman,

one's heuristic prerogative,

kinematic non-locality,

visionary pack-animals

coalesce a

radial union of open sets

On the convex…a

father was enfolded,

pianism in his leaf-like swim the

voices of camels echo up the walls a

Chevy we can borrow, .. two

men cutting a melon with a feather a

blind masseur at work on the

shoulders

of an actor

On the flat,

family narcissism a

tour de force of fanatical piety the

sun was playing with the rug, . . writ-

ten in a stream with a

suspended arm

On the convex…in true,

spent on light

when they met it,

drinking farewell tea in the

apricot garden the

eroticized gesture of licking the

paper a

banquet at which

ghost stories are told,

sprayed the heads of their gargoyles,

given a ray

in their cupped hands

While on yet another flat…

turning fear into architecture a

naked man crawling away up a hill a

cape-conscious Catalan begging for a cello

how

to trivialize a room, . . un-

diminished ink

thrilled through

Now on convex...

moss on snow in-

completeness and dynamism

are one the

first, who frayed the end of a reed, es-

chewing envy with her foot,

lost

in thought .. numinous avifauna twang

and covey on a slender

eucalyptus an

invitation to reclusion

amongst

steams and shade hills the

beguiling nature of our emotional en-

velopes .. gone are mannerly utopias that

refuse themselves,

love that meets

Still on the flat…

by me, by many, by nearly all a

midwayer pile-driven to poverty,

home-life resentment .. what

undid us ..

a mother dies before a child wakes,

earning and darkness,

parting by death from wind,

descending after asceticism,

came to sticky ends

by his own entourage

Further, on convex, spherily

sitting beneath the fig

systems of belief portrayed as knowledge a

fuchsia dell,

what

the light said,

carp ascend a

waterfall

poets ache for each other o-

palescent sulla and cardoon honey, an

old reptilian tree sprouts,

butterflies over waves,

fast beta-spindles

But on us evenly…

in *flagrante delicto*

which I am here muting…yes,

we labor under…for

already we have been

beneath our dignity,

~*infra-dig*

in blousy lie-mass

and stand out

~*ex-sistere*

we labor under

~*infimum*

greatest lower-bound

O eyes,

long and trenchant

rose above the debates

you I crave…

for I called to mind how

not Being but

something prior

to ferocity

and intractability of

beasts, therein…is the

closest thing to bare-

foot, therein shorter

than the violet end of visible light

When eyes slither up an arapahoeish moon,

mosquito-net yurt spread with summer quilts,

that is…on simple grounds of luminosity

we cross a ravine by way of a fallen pine-trunk,

water, wind, solar energy and peacefully split atoms

in our employ,

pleasures of emptiness and

absence of telo-numb theatrical gestures,

but if, then, one is the gloss of the other,

observer quandaries

we haven't the leisure to defeat,

shall it next press that loving to eve,

for here…evidence…an inchoate ear

is my hand smoldering and agape sits lightly upon us,

or rather…less

and less chthonic thrall,

release us

fee-simple

Concerning things we

have mentioned

from the beginning

the ulterior mouth of the

word

was pressed against

celestial gnaw

all

along, the beam starts as a

featureless clump,

originates in unbound energy,

even so, *pari passu*, when

backing out of a cut, ask

a mortal a searching question...what

~are the limits of maturity?

Of the gaping at my bonfire, you

remember how we .. on

an unsullied flat…the

virulent transfer of wealth a

sort-of crayfish in hand an

aper of atomic weight versus abundance, dis-

mantled pressure and origin,

vigorously waved peace, as

so often…some, quit

trenchant sabots to hide their

feet almost rolling their

nostrils in the sand and

why, slap-dash Death may

not come to my rescue, she

is knowing me to suffer

Stabat Mater

Lofty and ignoble

accomplices of love-

lessness we

get clammy

gulled and ulcer-clipped

peevish on our couches now

a mania for artificial ruins de-

mentedly is wished upon

We drag on a life

go and forget or re-

trace and pour forth

hard by a sure heath, leaves

...leaves are but vat-red on vat-

red razors being flipped

over in the light

and so, o cartouches,

only yesterday, the sun traveled by

merest boat at night, a

scarab pushed the sun by day,

postulates

Being and the *Void*

True…when each of our arms are

full with Qi fields and

we sleep freely on

soft sand, *ecstases*, we…

finitudinally

could neigh out, but

so can wild presencing

or ownmost sedition of any girl

who inescapably hides nothing,

treasures up against, as

though more seemly than water all

pitiable abstractions unite be-

hind us, all close

brushes, all

flatter-power

Yet hourly quantify for

some say be-

cause of vissicitudinal force

en-isled suddenly

and secretly

but feel ourselves so-

licited and dis-

tracted our hearts led a-

way by a harsh h-

and and the heart un-

able to withdraw itself

Suppose there is truly no

openness before us

from here

on in if

things are loot, how ..

I ask ..

rotting Einsteinian universes

mind-fists and

kissers of swords, why

something has M or

is held constant

Perhaps..

Dore's throngs *fff* tremolando with

covered heads in

their origins from mercy, tell

what birth-throes and pan-

ic-stricken volleys, which

of its sacral self, in

suppurating shirts of blood shout-

ing intimacies that

they should ever feel wonder,

Ex Ante

according to what lies ahead

it is enough that

sapience before

all else piing and a-

loof under mocking fire, we,

disclosively welling up, shall

cling to nothing, tidal-

tugging on our ex-

cruciating wet rock, wrap-

ped in willow-splints

All the while

it remains upon

these lives every

life lived livid

at such we

cotton on…with

four toes attached to a plinth no

boy is holding a colossal leg, so

long as finger-breadths point-cluster fore-

feel and pool as cherry

blossoms do we

arch and plafond in, in

over-small potencies be-

cause had there been n-

o long-axis,

gestural baksheesh

elm-seed money

lily-root money

cicada or cigale money

wreath cent or

no miner's angel…

Our foveas converge on a…we

admit into ourselves

against gravity a

human hunch…yet

a languor follows…the

messier sciences

co-alit, who e-

verywhere at once

theirs and ours

intimates…

Being manipulated by an image

to keep off the profane touch

So with all that pisseth,

capitalism protected from

planetessimal gullies in outer space,

personification of Peace and Tragedy

leaning on a tree our

tawny bees, born apart,

the bastard Time…visas,

concurs and tinges places

from false and true vacuums

smearing perception in

in this way

our congealed will

to will,

net-net, more

spitting than speech its

forsaken teeth chattering with

cold and plunging in undue order

robbed of evanescence runs

home breathless

absente reo

the defendant

being absent

My Dear Brother Marat

My dear brother Marat,

The center holds.

We have encumbered…as there was a need to dispose first, the ecru organdy garden-hat and hood of one Charlotte Corday, and too, her phantoms who come toward us as flirting ones, thereby inextricably altering our history forevermore.. The way to the eyes. I too am abstentious, feeling myself a neutered thing, then itch and tumesce toward the taking of a veil…but those cosmologists and astrologers will not take their leave, plus…and I reluctantly confess this…I picked up a dervish.

On a side trip to Pushkin, in an august little city of parks where I sang all of Shostakovich's Preludes and Fugues while consulting on disintegrating onslaughts and Russian/Western marriage contracts, I loathed to leave behind the spectacular thunderstorms, the nabbed copter, your white birches….pelmeni, kvass and schi….my balalaika and that book kiosk at Nevskii Prospekt. Why be wanton?

Cleverness passes as insight when realistic tendencies become dominant, though there is more to this than outmuscling vodka, under-nuanced Marxisms and unleashing our vocabulary. Breed and weep. Consider... frontal geometry, voltage and current-time curves in the middle of the Third Opium War for a dimensionless model not fitting the rest of the canon; poisonously beautiful paradox, diverse and volatile, freedom of a masterpiece....ever inopportune.

But only a finitude is a piercing of the lights. We will fall under (n)either their rubric (n)or their chickweed….they that have no nemesis…. symmetrical, undoubting creatures caught in formulaic crud ups, pall, redacted melodramas and farces. In finessing where consciousness fades and in hopes of diplomacy addressed to emperors and true feelings, let us squeeze tea between our teeth thereby warding off said desecrater's invidious psy-ops. O Marat, who can feel so much and act like he feels, who illumines madness, the storm, its forest for superfluous men…. do not leave off your humiliated mystical life. That which *is* you. I give you my painted emu eggs and spice chest, Marat, for as you well know; the egg is considered to be the most ancient pagan token of resurrection which frees you from gore and depression, so to the uplifting accounts of unimaginable hope. The creation of an affect; the *making* of love. You may reflect on the reasons not to live (for you might induce us also), but only to conclude the finest thing to do is continue *of being*. Such 'together knowing'. You cannot not dispose of your incessance without my knowingness. I repeat.., you must not desert your smock.

Love hinders death.

Thrall

When obscenely further back…malefic

democracy broken open,

optionally steps through you

disappearing in the dips,

and the bourgeois body

pursued to the limits of faded money

wills not

to jump its shark

Impressed into   the radiation

a single torrential fusion

draws aside panoptic

collapse of time and space

by none

exacted with more rigor

We, who go through the day

as yet unmingled in ceaseless flux

all the dead darkness

skyward...working the vault

Others in ersatz, gibbous sanctums

fire inversions of fear gleaming

redemptive glee,

the cauteries..

O, chaosists,

disintegratingly whisper

dieu le veut! god wants it!

to favor vicious prelates

defence itself a

seemingly invulnerable lie

feeding upon entropies

and that labor..

there as here

delightful at death

Strip us out

first money,

then time

now intimacy

Through effort and cunning

and no other manacle than logic

we think we state the cause,

wandering the halls of any science

as if orgies of naming

shimmy the body

of everyone,

chaotic as an egg

all at sea   snatching

Esprit des bagatelles!

coagula!

whose nature it is to be one long want

dartle along the surface of a

frictionless ocean

Enring us

not as casuistries' pulsation

nor as fashions of ruling accidias,

it is this inanity, this tenacious feces

deciding for the world

behind custodies of

small and large sadisms

As if we could...

through the agency

of moral incontinence..

And to then

lay odorless

O, takers-in of the sublime

some call sheer lifelessness,

do not give way,

wild-rice flourishes in slow-flowing streams,

and summer lightning..

matutine..

knowing the cause of beauty in fruit,

or the bliss of melting love,

thoughts have mass..

Any of this dogs the XYZist, cacophonies and

boffo intellectual franchisees

can be but

lobby-fodder

exuders of poignant helplessness

will the scapegoatee never triumph or

shame the obliterating bloodier?

Even some poets

gently hate the world

blurring the dignities

foolish fire, misleading light

while isomorphic to capitalism-imperialism

does first embrace manifestations of

apish ditsy chichi gauzy glib tacky puerile profundities

even if ungermane…it lifted you

who pluck the word wasp from a lexicon

when the same is untouched by

the sap of a thing in snowy waste

In the stumbling that speaks for me

I say death to vanity,

solipsism's potency

let the pyrrhic

burning thorn

in deeper

Mercy above Justice

Lissa Wolsak Interviewed

The interview was conducted on "our shared electro-epistolary plane" in fits & starts across the winter of 2000/1. A continuing conversation, of which this is a formalized fragment, began in September 1998: there is no reason to suppose this has concluded.

.....

PS: So there's this Literary Radar and the folk from our generation start blipping all over the screen from about 1970 onwards. No Lissa Wolsak until 1994, "*The Garcia Family Co-Mercy.*" Did the radar miss something, were earlier sightings possible or is that (which in conversation you've described as "written too hastily") the beginning?

LW: "*Noyade*" was in **Front** magazine, guest edited by Lisa Robertson, 1990. Jeff Derksen published the first section of "*Co-Mercy*" in **Writing**, and a half-anonymous piece "*Orchard Sutra,*" appeared in **Barscheit Nation**, all written very ad hoc.

Hasty, because I have a romantic notion of deepening a work, oaking it. So far, I have not had that opportunity, but would wish to.

PS: In Peter Riley's first poem in the anthology "A Various Art," p. 299, we read:

I am from language and will return to language
and no one will know
what else I might have been

What language, what silences have you emerged from?

LW: That quote is exquisite. For me, to speak at all, is suspect, just as it is almost always suspect to speak under the constraints in linearity, where the main question is: which surface must I appear on? In my work I presume to move through that silence which linear language admits, its lack of fullness, its utter necessity, placing a slight emphasis on the grace/civilizade /intuition of one who interprets its urgency.

From silence of early and late dogmas, of duplicity, of closed human circuits, of refuge and resistance to cultural engulfment, of fixed and encrypted ideas and obliteration that also naturally inheres in the language, then of all that had gone before, and that which holds love in fear. Very much from the silence of reflection, strong wishes, autonomy, a vulnerable defence of being.

I am no more than a (in)decent magpie.

I vehemently see no reason to dumb-down the sheer and useful beauty of language. What ~of cultivating an ability to see in, *pre*-positionally through, of, with, the space between atoms, space less tyrannized. I know what to write because language lightens itself to reveal the pan-psychic shock/sleep of being alive, anatomies of collectivity/ possibility, *juste-milieu*...the lucre of subjectivity.

By the authority which I grant to myself, I work with what comes, that which presents. We corner language no more than love.

PS: If writing has indeed come late for you what else have you already been?

LW: Mother, adventuress, beekeeper, volunteer friend to imprisoned people, volunteer friend and bridge for severely challenged persons, surgical nurse, hotelier, impresario, and recently free-lance artisan of ikebana, and a goldsmith.

PS: What are the circumstances of being grabbed by language?

LW: At first it was a protracted series of personal traumas and deaths; I was insane with grief. At the time, I was auto-didactically studying intently, reading in depth, reflecting on apparencies, acausal events, developing interpretive acumens of literature, music, theology, ontology, epistemology, art, the natural world, on death, on opposites, on asymmetry.

Inconsolable, atomized, there began a flow of imaginative arms, and visual hearing. I traded my grand piano in for a pen. Significance began to present, occur to me through all senses, but language was the most intimate of the gravitations, most persistent, and the one through which matter/meaning seemed to appear, perhaps simply because of the longing to know, which is an extension, of sorts, a self-hurled moving of and in the fields. Words came very much the way I later saw Celan imply.

PS: You've mentioned the "family resemblance" phenomenon to me (writers sending books or recommendations they think you'll like based on perceived similarities with your work—I know this, I've joined that club). Who would you place on your family tree? (In trying to avoid the "hoary" influence question I thought we'd go for "affinities" instead).

LW: I have affinity for all those who have taken liberty, and for those who have set others free, who are deliberate, immersed, and make inspired, originary moves.

PS: Would you be insulted, honored or indifferent to be tagged a latter-day "mystic"?

LW: I have and still do read from time to time matters pertaining to the Jewish, Buddhist, Christian and other mystical traditions, because they apprehended so much, were so ~on to things, the very same things that quantum physics is able to speak of now…but I am more of a flying veil. With respect to the abstruse, no one presides over the mysteries. I am wary of speciousness and much of what fuels talk. I do love insight and from early years have concerned myself with noumena, origins, cause/effect, acausality, action at a distance, synchronicity, useful self-captures, reflexivities, wanting to be in full contact with the nature of mind, and to rid myself of as many mediators of my ideas and experience as possible. I am resolutely interested in primary discourse and do not cultivate conventional formations of memory. My work is inflammatory, anti-clerical, anti-perfectionist, and a serious query into hatred/violence. 'Mystic' traces etymologically to the F. *mystérieuse*, and L. *mysterial*, to the Gr. *must-es* (close-mouthed). Contributory to must-es is m-uo, (I shut my mouth ((and close my eyes))). To speak/hear is to mercurially curve…I follow the incandescence but not ~only that; draw toward the equivocation of ethical spaces which well between intent and interpretation. Over-perturbed, words relinquish their autotelic, material usefulness, until we recreate or return them. On approach, some orders of matter recede, as they must, and further… depreciate or collapse in the observation. For me, it is important to understand the ~nature of the unsayable, keeping in mind the beauty and terror of an impossibility, and to work beside, as if it.., without the delusion that it can ever be fully apprehended in a way appealing to those who love proofs. We are precisely at the 'hard problem' of physicist fame. I tend to listen rather than speak, and through volition, refine my cognition, depth perception, sound/its absence, effortlessness and transfer of feeling.

PS: "To the poet, poetry is a vocation, it is the listening art. A line is an increment of nerve, an integer of grace."[Guy Birchard, "Birchard's Garage," Pig Press, p. 7] Certain key words of yours—"co-mercy," "transhumance"—seem to me entire nervous systems. Some remarks of yours once have made me want to vote for the skin as the organ of the soul.

Can you tease a question out of those remarks that you would like to curve some self out of?

LW: "Transhumance" had accrued through time, several definitions, but I waxed, elongated and grafted one in particular, from La Roy Ladurie's *Montaillou*, which had meant acts of rural economic symmetry, reciprocity and redistribution, to mean: social acts of symmetry, reciprocity and redistributions of generosity, forgiveness, love per se, and in doing so, ceasing or suspending the revenge cycle. It is, at bottom, an entirely different way of *aesthesis* (sensual consciousness). There is such enormous dynamism in these options.

"Co-mercy" is a coin intended to recoil from, and flip, in dissidence, the unvarying gluts of meaningless exchange, usury of supremacist commerce, and public/private cultural engulfment. If there is to be a revolution...let it be between us. Co-mercy at once proposes and oscillates in audacious disarmaments ~of all kinds~ by initiating and sustaining mercy in realization of our interconnected oneness, because we ~are the famous other. This short-circuits the often dubious act of waiting for the other to act first. Co-mercy contains the fragrance of surprise, forgiveness of debt, radiates from plein-air, fully potent, rather than from a plane..., and is an implicate footpath into the present/presence of I / Thou.

PS: Your quarrel with linearity seems profound. Do you have a sense of the roots of that mistrust for you? Do you have any inklings of where else this might lead you in terms of shape and form—in writing and living?

LW: I have an antipathy toward flatland embrittlements within normative sentence making because I have not often enough experienced the truth of their/my constructions. Moreover, the mind is non-local and undermines my smooth to the eye approaches. I choose, rather, to activate consciousness, and to keep a loose hold on the smoky, beguiling and sometime fatuous muse of controlled meaning, but not to exclude the genuinely intended or navigable. I am more a receiver of shape and form than an architect of same. By its very facture, I write to surprise myself.

LaVergne, TN USA
06 June 2010
185151LV00002B/4/P